The Truth About
ISLAM &
JIHAD

John Ankerberg
Emir Caner

QUR'AN. COM

HARVEST HOUSE PUBLISHERS

EUGENE, OREGON

Cover by Dugan Design Group, Bloomington, Minnesota

Cover photos © Roberto A. Sanchez / iStockphoto; StockXpert

THE TRUTH ABOUT ISLAM AND JIHAD
The Truth About Islam Series
Copyright © 2009 by John Ankerberg and Emir Caner
Published by Harvest House Publishers
Eugene, Oregon 97402
www.harvesthousepublishers.com

Library of Congress Cataloging-in-Publication Data
    Ankerberg, John, 1945-
    The truth about Islam and jihad / John Ankerberg and Emir Caner.
       p. cm.
    Includes bibliographical references.
    ISBN 978-0-7369-2501-3 (pbk.)
    1. Jihad. I. Caner, Emir Fethi. II. Title.
    BP182.A54 2009
    297.7'2—dc22

2008046373

Printed in the United States of America

09 10 11 12 13 14 15 16 17 / VP-SK / 10 9 8 7 6 5 4 3 2

Contents

Section Five
Jihad As Carried Forward by Muhammad's Early Successors

Section Six
Jihad from Islam's Greatest Years to the Present

Section Seven
Our Response to Jihad

Section Eight
Conclusion

A Guide to Arabic Terms and Abbreviations

Though many of the Arabic words used in this book are described in their context, a few foundational terms are noted here to help explain what you may encounter in these pages. The version of the Qur'an used in this book, unless otherwise indicated, is the translation of Mohammed Pickthall,* considered one of the most authoritative versions among English-speaking Muslims.

Bukhari: Named after its compiler, Muhammad ibn Ismail al-Bukhari, this *Hadith* (collection of reports about Muhammad) is the most respected compilation within the *Sunna,* the body of practice and custom based on Muhammad's words and deeds.

Caliph (also *calif*): The title of Islamic leaders after Muhammad's death. Among the Shiites, caliphs have been replaced by *imams*.

Five Pillars: The five foundational spiritual practices in Islam required of all Muslims in order to enter Paradise.

Hadith: "Story" or "report": collection of sayings and examples of Muhammad; highest Islamic authority after the Qur'an.

Hajj: One of the five pillars of Islam. It commands all Muslims able to do so to visit the Muslim holy site in Mecca at least once during their lifetime.

Hijra (English, *hegira*): Literally, "departure": the flight of Muhammad and his followers from Mecca to Medina in AD 622.

---

* Mohammed Marmaduke Pickthall, tr., *The Meaning of the Glorious Quran.*

Imam: A Muslim holy leader, usually in charge of a local mosque. In Shiite Islam, a supreme spiritual guide who is a direct descendant of Ali, and thus Muhammad.

Jihad: An Arabic term for "resistance," interpreted as a spiritual struggle or as an external struggle (violence and war).

Kafir (plural, *kuffar*): An infidel; a disbeliever in Allah.

Mecca: Islam's most holy site, which all able Muslims must visit at least once during their lifetime.

Mosque: A building in which Muslims hold prayers and worship activities.

Mujahid (plural, *mujahidin*): A holy warrior; one who fights for Islam.

Muslim: One of the most respected (*sahih*) compilations of the words and deeds of Muhammad (the *Sunna*), this collection, named for its compiler, Muslim ibn al-Hajjaj, contains about 4,000 traditions (*ahadith*).

Qur'an: The holy book of Muslims, said to contain, word for word, the instruction Allah gave to Muhammad, the founder of Islam.

Shia: Literally, "faction." *Shiite* has come to mean a "follower of Ali"—one who believes the caliph Ali was the true successor to Muhammad.

Sunni: "People of the Way." Followers of Abu Bakr and Umar, the first two caliphs, as successors to Muhammad.

Sura (sometimes *surah*): The name used for each section of the Qur'an; equivalent to "chapters" in reference to the Bible.

Umma: The Islamic community; the community of believers in Allah.

Introduction: The Question of Peace or Violence

And fight them until persecution is no more, and religion is for Allah.

—Sura 2:193

Jihad, viewed as synonymous with "holy war," is a word that has brought fear and concern to millions in the West during recent years. Seen through the lenses of the 9/11 attacks of 2001, the Madrid train bombings of 2004, and the London bombings of 2005 (also known as the 7/7 bombings), jihad has become indistinguishable from militant Islam's insatiable and merciless war against Western democracies. These societies, due to their staunch belief in political freedom, are in fact regarded by Islamists as putrid enablers of immorality who wish to export their sins to Muslims throughout the world.

However, the aggressive war waged against the West is only one front on which the Islamists fight. These purist Muslims are also waging battle against an internal foe known as infidels (Arabic, *kuffar*). *Infidels* are defined simply as those who were born Muslim and convert to some other faith.

More than any others, it is these men and women who are most likely to find themselves at the wrong end of a Muslim sword or rifle. Is it not ironic that these people—the ones closest to and embedded in Muslim culture—are themselves the most prone to have their blood shed by those who believe it is their duty to rid their societies of corruption and wickedness?

1

What has been the experience of people under Islam's rule?

Those who persecute infidels take action based on the words of their founding prophet, Muhammad, who declared, "If a Muslim changes his Islamic religion, kill him" (Bukhari 9.57). Thus, when asking whether Islam is a religion of peace or violence, one approach is to view that question through the eyes of a person who was part of that system and then rejected it.

Consider the Muslim convert from Judaism who was executed by the order of Muhammad for reverting to his previous faith. The account is found within the second sacred text of Islam, known as the *Hadith* (traditions):

> Behold: There was a fettered man beside Abu Muisa. Mu'adh asked, "Who is this (man)?" Abu Muisa said, "He was a Jew and became a Muslim and then reverted back to Judaism." Then Abu Muisa requested Mu'adh to sit down but Mu'adh said, "I will not sit down till he has been killed. This is the judgment of Allah and His Apostle['] (for such cases) and repeated it thrice. Then Abu Musa ordered that the man be killed, and he was killed. Abu Musa added, "Then we discussed the night prayers and one of us said, 'I pray and sleep, and I hope that Allah will reward me for my sleep as well as for my prayers.'"[1]

This story is remarkable for numerous reasons, not the least of which is the effortlessness with which Muhammad's confidants take someone's life. Additionally, the two Muslim lieutenants, after the bloodletting, simply sit down to dinner and discuss the religious issues of the day. They matter-of-factly share their hopes for eternal rewards, all the while indifferent to the fate of the Jewish man, who, according to their own doctrine, they have doomed to unending torture in the lowest part of hell.

Consider a young Arab boy whose story is both unique and tragic.

Geronimo, born in 1534, was sold as a slave to a Spaniard when he was four years old, raised a Catholic until he was about eight, and then escaped and returned home to once again avow Islam. In 1559, at age 25, Geronimo determined to revert to Christianity. He returned to his old master, with whom he gained favor, and enlisted in a Spanish squadron. Ten years later he was captured while on an expedition and given an ultimatum: recant Christianity or die.

> "We shall not manifest our religion publicly nor convert anyone to it. We shall not prevent any of our kin from entering Islam."

Samuel Zwemer, the pioneer missionary to Muslims in the nineteenth century, tells the final events of Geronimo's life:

> The Pasha [lord] was then engaged in building a fort called the Burj-Seti-Takelilt...to protect the water-gate...of Algiers. On September 18th, A.D. 1569, Geronimo was sent for and given the choice of either at once renouncing Christianity, or being buried alive...But the faith of Geronimo was not to be shaken. The chains were then struck off his legs, he was bound hand and foot, and thrown into the case of concrete. A Spanish renegade called Tamango, who had become a Moslem under the name of Jaffar, leapt in upon him, and with his heavy mallet hammered him down into the concrete. The block was then built up into the north wall of the fort.[2]

Nearly 300 years later, in 1853, the bones of Geronimo were uncovered and placed in a chapel. The martyr's hands were still bound, but "in the awful struggles of suffocation his legs had broken loose."[3]

We can also view the question of Islam's peacefulness through the eyes of non-Muslims who are forced to live under its control. Consider the Syrian Christians who were conquered by the Muslim hordes in the seventh century and forced to sign a surrender treaty, known as the Pact of Umar. This accord, named after the second leader of Islam after Muhammad's death, illustrates well the oppression that came with Islam as it began its conquest of the civilized world. It denotes in part the laws Christians would be required to keep:

We shall not build, in our cities or in their neighborhood, new monasteries, Churches, convents, or monks' cells, nor shall we repair, by day or by night, such of them as fall in ruins or are situated in the quarters of the Muslims.

We shall not manifest our religion publicly nor convert anyone to it. We shall not prevent any of our kin from entering Islam if they wish it.

We shall show respect toward the Muslims, and we shall rise from our seats when they wish to sit.

We shall not display our crosses or our books in the roads or markets of the Muslims. We shall use only clappers [bells] in our churches very softly. We shall not raise our voices when following our dead. We shall not show lights on any of the roads of the Muslims or in their markets. We shall not bury our dead near the Muslims.

If we in any way violate these undertakings for which we ourselves stand surety, we forfeit our covenant [*dhimma*], and we become liable to the penalties for contumacy [rebelliousness toward authority] and sedition.[4]

This meticulously worded document ensures the persecution of Christians. Though it makes them a protected class, they are a second-class citizenry—and if they express their faith according to the mandates of their own sacred text, they are considered seditionists worthy of death according to the Qur'an. The only question left to ask is, "What will be the mode of the traitor's execution?" After all, sura 5:33 allows for beheading or crucifixion.

This formative document has been the template for all other conquered lands—lands including all of North Africa, the Iberian Peninsula, and much of Asia. Though widely unknown, the Pact of Umar has held sway over the hearts and lives of more people than most other legal documents, and it finds its justification in the mind of Muhammad.

2

What can happen today to those who live under Islam's dictates?

Is Islam violent or peaceful? Consider a recent example. Fatima al-Mutairi, a 26-year-old Saudi woman, was executed in August 2008 by her own brother because of her conversion to Christ.

Wanting her family to find the same Truth she had found, Fatima boldly shared her newfound faith with them. Her brother, a member of Saudi Arabia's Commission of the Promotion of Virtue and Prevention of Vice, immediately went to her room and rummaged through the personal files on her computer to obtain the information needed to prove her "vice." As is commonly known, Saudi Arabia decrees the death penalty for anyone who renounces Islam.

Fatima was locked in her room for four hours, time she spent writing a poem entitled "And We for the Sake of Christ All Things Bear." She sent out this poem, her last letter, to friends via the Internet. Part of it reads,

> We left Mohammed, and we do not follow in his path
> We followed Jesus Christ, the Clear Truth
> Truly, we love our homeland, and we are not traitors
> We take pride that we are Saudi citizens
> How could we betray our homeland, our dear people?
> How could we, when for death—for Saudi Arabia—we stand ready?
> The homeland of my grandfathers, their glories, and odes—for it I am writing
> And we say, "We are proud, proud, proud to be Saudis"
> We chose our way, the way of the rightly guided
> And every man is free to choose any religion
> Be content to leave us to ourselves to be believers in Jesus
> Let us live in grace before our time comes
> There are tears on my cheek, and Oh! the heart is sad
> To those who become Christians, how you are so cruel!
> And the Messiah says, "Blessed are the Persecuted"
> And we for the sake of Christ all things bear

What is it to you that we are infidels?
You do not enter our graves, as if with us buried
Enough—your swords do not concern me, not evil nor disgrace
Your threats do not trouble me, and we are not afraid
And by God, I am unto death a Christian—Verily
I cry for what passed by, of a sad life.[5]

A few moments after Fatima finished writing this poem, her life was snuffed out by her own flesh and blood. Her brother acted in loyalty to his prophet and followed him well; Fatima acted on behalf of her Lord and finished well. Although she lived in what is perhaps the most oppressed nation on earth, she not only understood true freedom...as the poem indicates, she *found* true freedom.

☪

Is Islam a religion of peace? You decide. And we haven't even begun to discuss the issue of military engagement, which will offer much more evidence to consider.

The Definition of Jihad in the Qur'an and the Traditions

Those who were left behind rejoiced at sitting still behind the messenger of Allah, and were averse to striving with their wealth and their lives in Allah's way. And they said: Go not forth in the heat!
Say: The fire of hell is more intense of heat, if they but understood

— SURA 9:81, EMPHASIS ADDED —

At some point, all people, regardless of religious or political affili-ation, grow weary of war. That was the case after World War I, when Turkey was led from its Islamic roots into Western modernity by Mus-tafa Kemal Atatürk (1881–1938). The once great Ottoman Empire, centered in Turkey, had guided Islam for the past four centuries but was brought to its knees after the Great War. Atatürk's reforms, begun after the Turkish War of Independence ended in 1923, were nothing short of miraculous: The nation embraced democracy and rejected tra-ditional Islamic politics.

But what caused such unprecedented reforms? Simply put, Turks were tired of the violence. World War I had only brought pain and suffering. And the Turks themselves were responsible for the calcu-lated deaths of hundreds of thousands of Armenians (many of whom were Christians), who were hunted down, deported, and systematically executed for more than four years. After so much bloodshed, Turks were more than willing, through their own indigenous leadership, to correct their wayward path even if that meant rejecting long-held customs for newer, unfamiliar systems.

All things being equal, the secularization of Turkey should not have happened. Once a territory accepts Islam, it must remain part of the Islamic community (*umma*) forever. It is unimaginable to many Muslims that they would lose ground, when Muslims are called to be expansionistic in their faith.

The unimaginable changes in Turkey

Kemal Atatürk abolished the Islamic caliphate (leadership council) and Islamic law, banned many forms of Islamic clothing, and separated public education from Islamic schools and seminaries (*madrassas*). Moreover, women were given the right to vote, political freedom replaced sharia law, and Western rationalism was welcomed in areas such as philosophy and science. The nation accustomed to attacking Christian-dominated countries absorbed Western secularism and equality. The empire responsible for conquering one of the greatest Christian cities in the history of humanity, Constantinople, became the first Muslim nation-state ever to reject traditional Islamic politics. In a sense, Turkey became the standard-bearer for other Islamic countries that were contemplating political change.

As Bernard Lewis, perhaps the most respected Islamic scholar of the twentieth century, points out in his book *The Crisis of Islam*,

> In Muslim tradition, the world is divided into two houses: the House of Islam (*Dar al-Islam*), in which Muslim governments rule and Muslim law prevails, and the House of War (*Dar al-Harb*), the rest of the world, still inhabited and, more important, ruled by infidels.[1]

By democratizing itself, Turkey conceded that Muhammad's political system was flawed and that the way of the infidel was to be accepted.

It is no wonder why, as the verse at the beginning of this section points out, Allah threatens those who do not participate in violent jihad with the severest of punishments in the hereafter. Without such an admonition, many would choose to lay down their arms. But Islam prescribes endless conflict until such time as the world accepts Islam or at least bows to its laws (sura 9:33).

3

How is jihad actually defined?

*Sanction is given unto those who fight because they have
been wronged; and Allah is indeed Able to give them victory; those who have been driven from their homes
unjustly only because they said: Our Lord is Allah.*

—SURA 22:39

Sura 22:39 is traditionally considered the first verse to command
war against unbelievers, according to world-renowned Islamic scholar
Rudolph Peters. Indeed, the Qur'an is laden with references to holy
war and "frequently mentions jihad and fighting (*qital*) against the
unbelievers."[2] Peters defines *jihad*—the root of which means "to strive,
to exert oneself, to struggle"—as including at least four features:[3]

- An endeavor towards a praiseworthy aim
- A struggle against one's evil inclinations
- An exertion for the sake of Islam and the *umma* [community]—
  for example, trying to convert unbelievers or working for the
  moral betterment of Islamic society
- An armed struggle against the unbelievers

Expanding on his definition, Peters notes that jihad may take peaceful
forms (*greater jihad,* or *jihad of the soul*) or bloody forms (*lesser jihad,*
or *jihad of the sword*).

Furthermore, jihad finds its origins not only in the militancy of
Muhammad but in the culture of pre-Islamic Arabia. Since custom
allowed Arabian tribes to fight any other tribe with which they did not
have a binding truce, war was permissible whether it was resistance
against aggression or an attempt at conquering territory.

The bottom line is that Muslims, accepting the cultural norms of the
Arabian Peninsula and the example of their founder, have believed they
have every right to attack nonbelievers until the time a truce is reached

between both parties. And, as noted above, the lofty goal of conquering unbelieving lands and peoples, jihad of the sword, is a "praiseworthy aim" equal to conquering spiritual evil, jihad of the soul.[4]

4

Doesn't the Qur'an exclusively teach defensive war?

> *Fight in the way of Allah against those who fight against you,*
> *but begin not hostilities. Lo! Allah loveth not aggressors.*
>
> —SURA 2:190

Muslim apologists will quickly cite the verse above as proof that the Qur'an does not legitimize aggression unless Muslims are first wronged. It is evident, they argue, that the Qur'an puts forth a similar view of war as is found in the New Testament. However, upon closer examination, nothing can be further from the truth.

First, we must realize that Muhammad proclaimed tolerance while Muslims were a minority in Mecca. But when he seized power in Medina after the *hijra* (the flight from Mecca), verses like the one above took a backseat. Bernard Lewis explains the shift in *jihad's* meaning:

> When the Prophet was still a leader of a minority group and struggled against the dominant pagan oligarchy, the word often has the meaning...of moral striving. In the later chapters [of the Qur'an], promulgated in Medina, where the Prophet headed the state and commanded its army, it usually has a more explicitly practical connotation. In many, the military meaning is unequivocal.[5]

Second, the Bible never allows for unconditional war or a crusading mentality (see Romans 12:18). However, the Qur'an explicitly condones this kind of conflict:

> Then, when the sacred months have passed, slay the idolaters wherever ye find them, and take them (captive), and besiege them, and prepare for them each ambush (sura 9:5).

Note once again that, unless a treaty has been signed, war is permissible and, indeed, praiseworthy. And Muslims who do not go to war are considered subordinate to those who fight Allah's cause (sura 4:95).

Third, war in Christian thought has the express purpose of securing peace (see 1 Timothy 2:2) and removing those who oppress and act wickedly (see Romans 13:1-7). But war in Islam is different both in its scope and purpose. The latter half of sura 9:5 commands, "But if they repent and establish worship and pay the poor-due, then leave their way free. Lo! Allah is Forgiving, Merciful."

As a result, Muslim armies must not put down their swords until the time their opposition submits to Islam or Islamic law—that is, until unbelievers either worship Allah or pay a special protection tax and acquiesce to an Islamic political system. For the devout Muslim, war has a divine purpose and a divine outcome—securing the territory in the name of Allah, to whom all must bow.[6]

After the enemy submits, the surrender treaty is considered forever binding. If at any time, years or even centuries after the treaty was accepted, a conquered party breaks it, war is to be waged until such time that Islamic law is fully reestablished. The Qur'an decrees,

> And if they break their pledges after their treaty (hath been made with you) and assail your religion, then fight the heads of disbelief—Lo! They have no binding oaths—in order that they may desist (sura 9:12).

Finally, the Qur'an's definition of who the enemy is and how they should be treated is diametrically opposite to Christian teachings. Christians are commanded to love their enemy (Matthew 5:44), even when those enemies persecute them. In Islam, the enemy is defined as the infidel—the non-Muslim who lives in immorality and ignorance. Infidels by definition inhabit the "House of War," which must be reclaimed in the name of Allah. Sura 9:29 confirms this:

Fight against such of those who have been given the Scripture as believe not in Allah nor the Last Day, and forbid not that which Allah hath forbidden by His messenger, and follow not the Religion of Truth, until they pay the tribute readily, being brought low.

Islam delineates four enemies—"infidels, apostates, rebels, and bandits"[7]—as Lewis points out. Unconditional war is thus waged on those who rebel against the balance of the Muslim community. That rebellion can take two forms: *rational-spiritual* rebellion, as is seen in unbelievers and former Muslim believers; or *societal-political* rebellion, as seen in traitors and criminals.

5

Does the Hadith encourage or discourage jihad?

O Prophet! Strive [jihad] against the disbelievers and the hypocrites, and be stern with them. Hell will be their home, a hapless journey's end.

—Sura 66:9

In the life of a Muslim, nothing stirs up obedience more than the words of the prophet, Muhammad. His sayings, collected and authenticated more than two centuries after his death, were compiled into a collection known as the *Hadith* (traditions). Of the six major collections in existence today, Bukhari's is the most respected.

The Hadith is unambiguous about the commands of war and its benefits. Bukhari devotes an entire book (book 52) within one of his volumes to jihad. Look at the following verses from Bukhari, their explanations, and the ramifications for those considering jihad:

1. *Jihad is one of the best deeds a person can perform.*

   I asked Allah's Apostle, "O Allah's Apostle! What is the best deed?" He replied, "To offer the prayers at their early stated fixed times." I asked, "What is next in goodness?" He replied, "To be good and dutiful to your parents." I further asked,

"What is next in goodness?" He replied, "To participate in Jihad in Allah's Cause" (4.41).

2. *Jihad is obligatory to all Muslims when they are called upon by a Muslim leader.*

   If you are called (by the Muslim ruler) for fighting, go forth immediately (4.42).

3. *Jihad guarantees heaven to the warrior who dies in battle.*

   Allah guarantees that He will admit the *Mujahid* in His Cause into Paradise if he is killed, otherwise He will return him to his home safely with rewards and war booty (4.46).

4. *Jihad is better than anything the world has to offer.*

   The Prophet said, "A single endeavor (of fighting) in Allah's Cause in the forenoon or in the afternoon is better than the world and whatever is in it" (4.50).

5. *Jihad is best exemplified in the life of Muhammad.* In the Battle of the Trench, Muhammad was responsible for beheading 600 to 800 Jews. The adolescent and adult men, who had agreed to accept an unknown verdict from one of Muhammad's leaders, were sentenced to death *en masse*:

   > Some people (i.e. the Jews of Bani bin Quraiza) agreed to accept the verdict of Sad bin Muadh so the Prophet sent for him (i.e. Sad bin Muadh). He came riding a donkey, and when he approached the Mosque, the Prophet said, "Get up for the best amongst you." or said, "Get up for your chief." Then the Prophet said, "O Sad! These people have agreed to accept your verdict." Sad said, "I judge that their warriors should be killed and their children and women should be taken as captives." The Prophet said, "You have given a judgment similar to Allah's Judgment (or the King's judgment)" (5.148, punctuation as in original).

With one callous verdict, all the adult males of an entire Jewish tribe were exterminated. Note that the Qur'an designates Muhammad as the "excellent exemplar" of the Islamic faith—the one who is to be followed (sura 33:21).

6. *Jihad is to be carried out against different religious groups.*

Allah's Apostle said, "The Hour will not be established until you fight with the Jews, and the stone behind which a Jew will be hiding will say, 'O Muslim! There is a Jew hiding behind me, so kill him'" (4.177).

When it was the day of the battle of Al-Ahzab (i.e. the clans), Allah's Apostle said, "O Allah! Fill their (that is the infidels') houses and graves with fire as they busied us so much that we did not perform the prayer (that is 'Asr) till the sun set" (4.182).

7. *Jihad is followed by worship, thanking Allah for success.*

When the Prophet returned (from Jihad), he would say *Takbir* [glorifying Allah by saying, "God is Great"] thrice and add, "We are returning, if Allah wishes, with repentance and worshipping and praising (our Lord) and prostrating ourselves before our Lord. Allah fulfilled His Promise and helped His Slave, and He Alone defeated the (infidel) clans" (4.317).

In summary, jihad is defined as one of the greatest of all deeds, one that is obligatory to all Muslims; it is an act greater than the world itself and everything in it. It is to be carried out on different religious groups and end with the worship of Allah after success is secured. Jihad is, from beginning to end, a religious duty that finds its justification in the mind and life of Muhammad. The definitive meaning of jihad is found not within a text, but within a person.

The Rules of Jihad

The breaking story that flashes across the bottom of the screen has become routine on today's 24-hour-a-day news networks. Another homicide bomber has carried out a merciless, carefully plotted attack upon a crowd of unsuspecting shoppers. But then an entirely new twist is added to an already inhuman incident. Two mentally retarded women, later verified to have Down syndrome, were carrying the explosives and were then blown up in two crowded marketplaces in Baghdad.

After further investigation, it appears these two women were victims of an intentional al-Qaeda plot. Using bombers the public would overlook, the terrorists inflicted mass carnage using remote-detonated bombs. One reporter called the event "a scene straight out of the worst days of the [Iraq] conflict. Firefighters scooped up debris scattered among pools of blood, clothing and pigeon carcasses."[1] At least 73 people were killed, and hundreds of others were wounded in a scene that has become all too familiar to the viewing public.

Once again, people began asking who could plan such savagery. Are such actions in any way connected with Islam or Islamic tradition? Do the Qur'an and Hadith condone or condemn violence in this form or any other form? If they condone it, is it not tragic and ironic that these attacks affect Muslims more than Westerners? Additionally, why does this kind of violence seem to be so common in Islam in comparison to other religions, such as Christianity, Judaism, and Buddhism?

In an age of religious illiteracy and confusion, any answers to these questions, in order to be trusted, must be judged according to the original sources of Islam.

6

Who can call a jihad?

*O ye who believe! Obey Allah, and obey the messenger and those of
you who are in authority; and if ye have a dispute concerning any
matter, refer it to Allah and the messenger if ye are (in truth) believers
in Allah and the Last Day. That is better and more seemly in the end.*

—Sura 4:59

During the formative years of Islam, it was easy to understand who
could declare war against an enemy. While alive, Muhammad was the
sole authority and leader (*caliph*) in Islam; after him, there was a clear suc-
cession of rulers, the first four of which were
known as the "Rightly Guided Caliphs."
Although a splinter branch of Islam known
as the *Shia,* or party of Ali, formed around
the principle that the next leader of Islam
should be related to Muhammad, the vast
majority of the Muslim community followed the leader who was chosen by the
people. Even as Islam developed and power was extended to different
regions and groups, a clear leader usually emerged. This allowed worldwide jihad to continue to advance.

> Enough ambiguity exists
> to allow a place for the
> chaos and terrorism
> that ensnares much of
> the world presently.

This situation was largely the case until the rise of colonialism in the
eighteenth century divided the house of Islam. Then the abolishment
of the Caliphate (Islamic Leadership Council) in the twentieth century
destroyed the political infrastructure of Islam (see sidebar on page 14).
In the aftermath of these changes, decisions about war were given over
to the leaders of the tribes or nations.

But a quandary came about. If an infidel nation had taken possession
of a former Muslim stronghold, thereby removing their legitimate ruler,
was jihad to be forsaken? Or was the responsibility of jihadic declaration
assigned to someone else? Traditional wisdom asserted that Muslims
should rise up and reclaim what was rightly theirs and fight to usher in
a new reign of peace and justice.

Moreover—and very significant for today's situation—if Muslims had the right to declare jihad in former Muslim states, then why would it not be justifiable to declare war in territories *yet to submit* to Islamic rule? Although the majority of Muslim scholars agree that jihad should be declared by a political leader of Islam, enough ambiguity exists to allow a place for the chaos and terrorism that ensnares much of the world presently.[2]

NB

7

Is jihad mandatory or voluntary?

Warfare is ordained for you, though it is hateful unto you; but it may happen that ye hate a thing which is good for you, and it may happen that ye love a thing which is bad for you. Allah knoweth, ye know not.

—SURA 2:216

Averroës (1126–1198, also known as Ibn-Rushd), a judge and probably the most respected and famed medieval Islamic scholar, stipulated the traditional and historical view on jihad. In his legal handbook, *Al-Bidaya,* he concluded, "Scholars agree that the jihad is a collective not a personal obligation...the Prophet never went to battle without leaving some people behind."[3]

The basis for this conclusion is found in the verse quoted above as well as in sura 9:122:

> And the believers should not all go out to fight. Of every troop of them, a party only should go forth, that they (who are left behind) may gain sound knowledge in religion, and that they may warn their folk when they return to them, so that they may beware.

Based on these verses, four conclusions can be made.

1. Traditional Islamic theology equated jihad and military battle,

a comparison that was based in nothing less than the life of their prophet.

2. This belief about militant jihad held *near unanimity* until modern times.

3. When an Islamic ruler called Muslims to battle, there was no another option but to follow his command.

4. Finally, those left behind were not mere spectators. They were called to be a stronghold of Islamic belief and sustain Islamic law in the region already conquered.

8

Who is required to participate?

There is no blame for the blind, nor is there blame for the lame, nor is there blame for the sick (that they go not forth to war). And whoso obeys Allah and His messenger, He will make him enter Gardens underneath which rivers flow; and whoso turns back, him will He punish with a painful doom.

—SURA 48:17

According to Averroës, those obligated to participate in jihad are "adult free men who have the means at their disposal to go to war and who are healthy, that is, not ill or suffering from chronic diseases."[4]

Women, however, are not obliged to enter into war. As the Hadith relates, Aisha, the youngest wife of Muhammad, approached him with a question:

> ..."O Allah's Apostle! We consider Jihad as the best deed. Should we not fight in Allah's Cause?" He said, "The best Jihad (for women) is Hajj-Mabrur (that is, Hajj [pilgrimage to Mecca] which is done according to the Prophet's tradition and is accepted by Allah)" (Bukhari 4.43).

Finally, parents must release their children to go to war.

> A man came to the Prophet asking his permission to take part in Jihad. The Prophet asked him, "Are your parents alive?" He replied in the affirmative. The Prophet said to him, "Then exert yourself in their service" (Bukhari 4.248).

However, it is well known that women, who were not obligated in jihad, still fought in what were considered the noblest battles of formative Islam. In fact, women took part in many expeditions even though it was not mandatory. (It is important to note that those who were not required to fight were not forbidden to fight either.)

Islam's women warriors

Here are some examples of women who fought in military engagements:

- Umm Sulaym bint Milhan fought along with Muhammad's army and was known at one point for carrying a dagger in the folds of her dress.

- Aisha, Muhammad's wife, guided forces into battle against the fourth leader of Islam, Ali.

- During the conquest of Damascus, a few years after Muhammad's death, the daughter of the chief of the Arab Himar tribe defended her mortally wounded father and shot the Greek governor, Thomas, through the eye.[5]

It was only after Islam developed into a world power and professionalized its military that women were placed in a thoroughly submissive role. The present-day rise of women jihadists does not reflect an "extreme" form of Islam, but rather a desire of some Muslim reformers to return to a seventh-century Islam.

9

Who is Islam's enemy?

*Fight them until there is no persecution and
the religion is God's entirely.**

—SURA 8:39

Averroës pointedly declares that "all polytheists should be fought."[6] Oddly, this single phrase makes up nearly his entire discussion of the question, "Who is the enemy of Islam?"—though he wrote an entire philosophical treatise related to the subject. That such an important question is treated so cursorily by a respected scholar clearly indicates that Islam was primarily an offensive religion. In other words, Islam believed it was only right that the world should come under the sway of the prophet's declarations.

Further, since Averroës saw no need to give more than a brief answer, this indicates that Muslims unanimously agreed with the classic definition—that polytheists, the worst of all creatures (sura 98:6), must be defeated for the betterment of the world and the advancement of Islam.

During the formative years of Islam, Arabia was heavily dominated by polytheists. Hence, the enemy was easily defined. These pagans controlled Muhammad's hometown of Mecca. They worshiped the 360 idols found within the Kaaba, the cubical structure that enshrined polytheism and received thousands of pagan pilgrims each year. In time, Muhammad conquered the city, destroyed the idols (though not the Kaaba), and re-established monotheistic worship.

Muhammad, believing he was called to restore pure monotheism, hoped to win over the monotheistic Jews and Christians while conquering pagans across the Arabian Peninsula. He eventually recognized the futility of his course and declared Jews and Christians enemies of the state as well:

---

* From A.J. Arberry, tr., *The Koran Interpreted.*

O ye who believe! Take not the Jews and the Christians for friends. They are friends one to another. He among you who takes them for friends is (one) of them. Lo! Allah guides not wrongdoing folk (sura 5:51).

Heretical Christians known as the Marianites were therefore perceived as polytheists because they worshipped Mary. Orthodox Christians were also categorized as polytheists (specifically, tritheists) since they worshipped God the Father, God the Son, and God the Holy Spirit (sura 4:171). *NB*

Christians were lumped together with Jews as corrupters of the one true God—Allah—and both were therefore deemed enemies of Allah's cause. They were treated somewhat differently than other polytheists, and they were given the right to exist as long as they paid a protection tax (sura 9:29) and the caliph saw fit to keep the treaty with them intact. Nonetheless, the two groups were subjected to harsh Islamic law and were made second-class citizens with far fewer rights than Muslims (as previously explained on pages 9–10).[7]

Ultimately, then, the enemy of Islam is defined as one who has not submitted to Islam and Allah, a definition from the Qur'an that encapsulates all nonbelievers.

10

When can war be declared?

Whosoever goeth right, it is only for (the good of) his own soul that he goeth right, and whosoever erreth, erreth only to its hurt. No laden soul can bear another's load. We never punish until we have sent a messenger.

—SURA 17:15

The Qur'an and Hadith assume that warfare is acceptable unless a truce has been declared. The only prerequisite for Muslims to go to war is that "the enemy must have heard the summons to Islam."[8] The specific details of the summons are clearly outlined in the Hadith:

> When you will encounter your polytheist foes, then summon them to three things. Accept that which they consent to and refrain from [attacking] them. Summon them to conversion to Islam. If they consent to that, accept it and refrain from [attacking] them. Summon them thereupon to sally forth from their territory to the Abode of the Emigrants and impart to them that, if they do so, they will have the same rights and duties as the Emigrants.
>
> If they are unwilling to do so, however, and prefer to remain in their own territory, impart to them thereupon that they will be like the converted Bedouins, who are subject to the same supreme authority of God as the [other] believers, but who are not entitled to share in the spoils, unless they join the Muslims in the war. If they refuse that, then summon them to payment of poll-tax. If they consent to that, accept it and refrain from [attacking] them. But if they refuse it, then invoke the help of God and attack them.[9]

The crusade mentality is clearly seen in the above tradition. Muslims are overt aggressors who warn the enemy before bloodshed ensues. The enemy has two choices: convert or submit. In this regard, Osama bin Laden, who announced his intentions to go to war with America and her allies on February 23, 1998, strictly adhered to Islamic prerequisites for war. Ironically, Muhammad himself did not follow this dictate. As in other areas of his life that were not in line with his words, Muhammad was given special revelations that overrode his own commands.[10]

11

What is promised to those who fight in jihad?

The Prophet said, "The person who participates in (Holy battles) in Allah's cause and nothing compels him to do so except belief in

Allah and His Apostles, will be recompensed by Allah either with a reward, or booty (if he survives) or will be admitted to Paradise (if he is killed in the battle as a martyr). Had I not found it difficult for my followers, then I would not remain behind any sariya [troop] going for Jihad and I would have loved to be martyred in Allah's cause and then made alive, and then martyred and then made alive, and then again martyred in His cause."

—BUKHARI 1.35

Most Westerners have become familiar with the promise of virgins for those who die in jihad. This finds its source in a relatively unknown tradition passed down by Imam Tirmidhi (824–892), one of the six compilers of the Hadith. He wrote, "Mohammed said: 'The least reward for the people of paradise is 80,000 servants and 72 wives'" (Tirmidhi 2687).

A closer look at Muhammad's words reveals something not realized by most Westerners. According to Tirmidhi, Muhammad promised at least 72 virgins to *any* Muslim in heaven, not just for those who waged war on earth. This is confirmed by Allah's promises in the Qur'an: "Surely for the godfearing awaits a place of security…and maidens with swelling breasts, like of age" (sura 78:31,33).*

But to the average Muslim, who is not guaranteed heaven, the promise of virgins seems elusive. Muhammad himself was uncertain of his eternal destination (Bukhari 5.266). Every Muslim's fate is "fastened to his own neck" (sura 17:13) and is based on his own works (sura 23:101-103), and the will of Allah (sura 14:4).

The sole promise of eternal security in Islam is gained by those who die in jihad. The Qur'an exclaims,

> So those who fled and were driven forth from their homes and suffered damage for My cause, and fought and were slain, verily I shall remit their evil deeds from them and verily I shall bring them into Gardens underneath which rivers flow—a reward from Allah. And with Allah is the fairest of rewards (sura 3:195).

---

* From A.J. Arberry, tr., *The Koran Interpreted.*

The virgins spoken of so frequently are *guaranteed* for those who pay the ultimate price of war. The martyr can look forward to a heaven that provides pure spouses (sura 2:25), jeweled couches (sura 56:15), and fine wine (sura 56:18).

But eternal pleasures are not the only rewards of war. As the Bukhari Hadith relates above, Muslim conquerors are permitted to take booty of the enemy. That booty includes any and all items—buildings, weapons, food. No wonder chroniclers of early Islamic conquests, such as Sophronius, the patriarch of Jerusalem when it was conquered, recorded the Muslim invaders as "godless barbarians."[11] According to Ibn Warraq,

> Muslims burned churches, destroyed monasteries, profaned crosses, and horribly blasphemed against Christ and the church. In 639, thousands died as a result of the famine and the plague consequent to the destruction and pillage.[12]

Similar ruin occurred in Syria (634), Mesopotamia (635–642), and Egypt (642–643). The warriors who committed such atrocities were nearly all contemporaries of Muhammad…and they were simply carrying out the orders given to them through the prophet.

Islamic scholars disagree on the amount of destruction allowed upon an enemy. One tradition cautions, "Do not fell trees and do not demolish buildings." Yet Muhammad was known for such destruction, which places this tradition at variance with the example of the prophet. Since there is no clear prohibition of brutal destruction, and because of the harsh example of Muhammad, many Muslims believe they have every right to burn down buildings, destroy vegetation, and leave an area desolate.

"It is not for any prophet to have captives until he hath made slaughter in the land."

The Muslim conquerors brought with them, according to one eyewitness of the events, "extermination, ruin, and slavery."[13] But were these events consistent with the mandates of the Qur'an? Most definitely. Extermination of enemies finds its roots within the Qur'an, which explains, "It is not for any prophet to have captives until he hath made slaughter in the land" (sura 8:67).

However, some verses in the Qur'an encourage slavery as the kinder and more proper treatment of captives:

> Now when ye meet in battle those who disbelieve, then it is smiting of the necks until, when ye have routed them, then making fast of bonds; and afterward either grace or ransom till the war lay down its burdens (sura 47:4).

Regardless, the Qur'an clearly decrees either slavery or extermination for those who are defeated.

Is anyone safe from the brutalities of Islamic jihad? According to a consensus of Muslim scholars, some groups, including hermits, the aged, crippled, children, and noncombatant women are.[14] However, one of the major schools of Islamic thought, the Shafii school, argues that, on the basis of sura 9:5, *all* enemies—not just warriors—must be killed if they do not believe in Allah. Thus, in places where this school of thought dominates, such as Egypt and Indonesia, no infidel is safe from the sword of the Muslim if holy war is declared on the land.

Finally, the promise of booty was not confined to material things. It extended to people as well. Muhammad himself took women as spoils of war, as the Qur'an declares:

> O Prophet! Lo! We have made lawful unto thee thy wives unto whom thou hast paid their dowries, and those whom thy right hand possesses of those whom Allah hath given thee as spoils of war (sura 33:50).

Following their prophet's example, Muslim warriors considered it part of Allah's blessings to take conquered women as their wives. These concubines were considered possessions (sura 23:6) and commodities that could be used for compensation (sura 4:92). The Qur'an did limit what could be done with women slaves, prohibiting forced prostitution (sura 24:33) and encouraging their emancipation if they were virtuous in character (sura 90:12-13). Nonetheless, slaves were a reward from Allah for fighting in his cause, and the Qur'an teaches that they even follow martyrs to heaven as a reward (sura 76:19).[15]

Therefore, even in the final abode of heaven, there are those who are not free, but are enslaved to Muslims. Islam—a religion that promises peace and justice—promotes slavery in paradise, that perfect state of everlasting happiness (sura 39:73).

Muhammad's Understanding of Jihad

In September 2005, the conservative Danish newspaper *Jyllands-Posten* published a dozen controversial cartoons of Islam and its prophet. One stick-figure depiction had a brief rhyme attached: "Prophet, you crazy bloke! Keeping women under yoke!" Millions of outraged Muslims denounced the egregious insults to Islam and demanded proper punishment for the violators of moral decency. Muslims took to the streets, burned Western flags, and demanded action. One protestor exclaimed, "We demand that the Danish government make a clear and public apology for the wrongful crime."[1] Crime? What was the crime? And if it was a crime, what should be the punishment?

Westerners who are puzzled by the Muslim mentality should investigate the life and actions of Muhammad to better understand why Muslim reaction to the cartoons was so extreme. To the average Muslim, their response was not extreme; it was "exemplary." Why? Muslims, obeying the command of the Qur'an to imitate the prophet's actions (sura 33:21), did exactly what Muhammad had done. He denounced verbal insults against Islam and demanded severe punishment for those who ventured upon religious criticism, sarcasm, or derision.

On one occasion, Muhammad called for the assassination of a poetess whose works criticized Islam and Muhammad. Muhammad Haykal, a biographer of Muhammad respected by Muslims worldwide, relates the event:

> Likewise, 'Asma', daughter of Marwan, of the tribe of Banu Umayyah ibn Zayd, used to insult Islam and the Prophet by encouraging bad feeling against the Muslims. The Battle of

Badr did not make her reconsider. One day, 'Umayr ibn 'Awf attacked her during the night while she was surrounded by her children, one of whom she was nursing. 'Umayr was weak of sight and had to grope for her. After removing the child from his victim, he killed her; he then proceeded to the Prophet and informed him of what he had done.

When her relatives returned from the funeral, they asked him whether he had killed her. "Indeed so," said 'Umayr, "You may fight me if you wish. By Him Who dominates my soul, if you should deny that she composed her abusive poetry, I would fight you until either you or I fall." It was this courage of 'Umayr that caused the Banu Khutmah, the tribe of 'Asma's husband, to turn to Islam. Having converted to Islam but fearing persecution at the hand of their fellow tribesmen, some of them had hidden their conversion. Henceforth, they no longer did so.[2]

Lessons abound from this execution sanctioned by Muhammad. Notice first that this woman was put to death simply because she created ill will, or "bad feeling," against Muslims. Second, she should have known better since Allah had demonstrated his power through a victory in the Battle of Badr. Third, the poetess was killed in front of her children without regard to their future and their need for their mother. Fourth, the murder was justified since the assassin advanced the cause of Islam. Indeed, his courage led to the conversion of fellow tribesmen of the murdered woman. In sum, jihad was endorsed upon those who posed either a physical or intellectual threat to Islam.

12

Muslim raiding: Did Muhammad justify it in the name of Islam?

They question thee (O Muhammad) with regard to warfare in the sacred month. Say: Warfare therein is a great (transgression), but

> *to turn (men) from the way of Allah, and to disbelieve in Him*
> *and in the Inviolable Place of Worship, and to expel His people*
> *thence, is a greater with Allah; for persecution is worse than kill-*
> *ing. And they will not cease from fighting against you till they*
> *have made you renegades from your religion, if they can.*
>
> —Sura 2:217

During the beginning years of Islam (AD 610–622), Muhammad was relatively unsuccessful in converting others. In order to advance his cause, he ordered raids as a way of retaliating against those who rejected Islam and fought against its expansion. He personally led three of these raids.

Getting money was another motive. However, the display of Islam's power was the driving force behind these raids. Christian apologists Norman Geisler and Abdul Saleeb explain, "Doubtless the purpose of these attacks was not only to obtain financial reward, but also to impress the Meccans with the growing power of the Muslim force."[3]

One early raid is especially important to consider. Muslim raiders, pretending to be pilgrims on their way to Mecca, met up with a caravan near Nakhlah that was returning to Mecca from a journey to Yemen. The raiders asked to join the group as fellow travelers. The pagan traders granted the request because it was a sacred month and, therefore, rules forbade the shedding of blood that would normally be expected. Eventually, the Muslims ambushed the members of the caravan, killing one, taking two others captive, and plundering their goods.

Muslims in Medina, where they had settled after the migration (*hijra*), reacted strongly. They realized that the pagan Meccans, due to this unprovoked aggression, were inevitably going to retaliate. In addition, the Muslim raiders had broken the sacred peace they had sworn to observe during holy months.

However, Muhammad once again received a special revelation. While acknowledging that the attack was inappropriate, the revelation justified it by declaring (as seen above with the killing of Asma), "For persecution is worse than killing." One scholar concludes as follows:

> Trivial as this incident was, it gave a blow to [the Meccans']
> prestige which they could not afford. From this moment
> they must have been planning how to "teach a lesson" to this
> upstart in Medina.[4]

Intentionally or unintentionally, Muhammad started his rise to
power by attacking a group of peaceful travelers. The only sin of the
victims was their connection with the ruling tribe in Arabia, something
that made them vulnerable to raiders who would lower their ethics in
order to gain prominence.

Moreover, the victims were made out to be representatives of religious oppressors. The earliest biography of Muhammad documents that
the prophet received a revelation—that the Meccans "used to seduce
the Muslim in his religion until they made him return to unbelief after
believing, and that is worse with God than killing."[5] Therefore, "God
relieved the Muslims of their anxiety in the matter, the apostle took the
caravan and the prisoners."[6] In war, lying to the enemy had been justified, and breaking truces was acceptable since the Muslims considered
themselves religiously oppressed.

13

Did Muhammad target Jews in jihad?

*And Allah repulsed the disbelievers in their wrath; they gained no
good. Allah averted their attack from the believers. Allah is ever
Strong, Mighty. And He brought those of the People of the Scripture who supported them down from their strongholds, and cast
panic into their hearts. Some ye slew, and ye made captive some.*

—Sura 33:25-26

Early on, Muhammad hoped to win over Jews and Christians to his
new movement. In fact, during the early years of Islam, Muslims prayed
toward Jerusalem (until Muhammad received revelation that they should

be facing the Kaaba in Mecca—Bukhari 2.143). Jews were regarded as "People of the Book," who had many commonalities with Islam. Medina itself had a large population of Jews. In time, they signed a treaty with Muhammad that allowed them equal rights with Muslims in exchange for political support. But the Jews did not warm toward converting to Islam and were eventually considered traitors who conspired with the archenemy, the Meccans.

Muhammad's opinion of the Jews hardened severely at the same time his power surged. On one occasion a prominent Jew of Medina by the name of Ka'b sarcastically mocked Muhammad—and paid the highest price for his scornful words. Muhammad put out a death warrant on the Jewish man and, as Geisler and Saleeb summarize it, "Four persons volunteered and shortly returned to Muhammad with Ka'b's head in their hands."[7]

Muhammad then issued the order, "Kill any Jew that falls into your power." The unfortunate Jewish merchant Ibn Sunayna, who traded with Muslims, was the first victim of this decree. He was killed at the hands of the Muslim zealot Muhayissa. Muhayissa was at first rebuked by his brother for the cruelty of his action, to which he responded, "Had the one who ordered me to kill him ordered me to kill you I would have cut your head off." His brother was so impressed that he immediately became a Muslim, exclaiming, "By God, a religion which can bring you this is marvelous."[8]

The Prophet's vengeance

During the period Muslims were centered in Medina,

> A Jew of the tribe Banu Kainuka played an indecent prank on a married Arab woman. As she was sitting at the marketplace he fastened the skirt of her dress upon her shoulder with a thorn. A Moslem killed the daring jester, and the Jews retaliated by killing the murderer. Mohammed locked the guilty tribe in its own quarters. After a period of siege they were forced to surrender, on the condition that all of their possessions should

pass into Mohammed's hands. They themselves were released
and moved to Syria.[9]

Muhammad used the actions of one individual as an excuse to exile an
entire tribe of Jews. Moreover, he stole all of their possessions.

Muhammad's hatred for the Jews culminated in a mass extermination (previously mentioned on page 19). The Meccans had laid siege
to Muhammad and the Muslims, only to retreat when they realized
they could not succeed in the strategy. In the aftermath, the Jews were
isolated from the Meccans and found themselves outnumbered by
3000 Muslim jihadists. Muhammad asserted that he was summoned
by the Angel Gabriel to attack the Jews and finally defeat these infidels
(Muslim 4370).[10]

What happened next is nothing short of appalling. Even though
the Jews surrendered without any full-scale battle, all men were to be
executed and all women and children enslaved. One chronicler describes
the scene:

> The sentence was carried out; the prisoners were led out in
> batches, beheaded on the edge of a trench which had been dug
> in the market-place, and thrown in. The execution of some
> 800 men occupied the whole day and went on far into the
> night. Only one Jew abjured his religion to save his life. The
> rest, after prayer and reading of the scriptures, went calmly
> to their death.[11]

Muhammad massacred all of the men and adolescent boys even
though he well knew who the leaders were and could have acted
mercifully. The prophet who spoke of the "god most merciful, most
compassionate" eradicated an entire tribe of Jews from Arabia.

14

How did Muhammad view victory and defeat?

*O Prophet! rouse the Believers to the fight. If there are twenty amongst you…they will vanquish two hundred; if a hundred, they will vanquish a thousand of the Unbelievers.**

—SURA 8:65

The Battle of Badr is the best known and most revered battle of the early years of Islam. In AD 624, Muslim forces, fresh from a successful raid that garnered Muhammad the equivalent of 50,000 dollars, were confronted by 950 Meccans, an army three times their size. A battle quickly ensued, and the Meccans were convincingly defeated.

Muhammad attributed the triumph to Allah's power and favor. In addition, he asserted that Allah had spoken to him, promising that Muslim warriors would have ten times the strength of their opponents (see the verse above).[12] The Muslims concluded Allah was on their side, they could not be defeated, and any superiority of the enemy would be outweighed by the favor of Allah. As long as they obeyed Muhammad and the revelation he received, defeat was not an option.

However, just one year later, the Battle of Uhud demonstrated that any disobedience to the prophet carried dire consequences if not corrected. Muslims were once again overcoming the Meccan enemy until "Muslim archers defied Muhammad's orders and assisted their beleaguered friends near them."[13] The Meccans immediately surrounded the archers and forced the Muslims to swiftly retreat. The Muslim army was thoroughly humbled, but they believed they would still be victorious once they regrouped and adhered to Muhammad's revelations. In time Islam conquered all of Arabia and began the military dominance that would last for centuries.

---

* From Abdullah Yusuf Ali, tr., *The Holy Quran.*

Today, millions of Muslims have the very same mentality. Although outnumbered by and less well equipped than their enemies, they believe Allah will smile upon their ventures once they return to the pure Islam of the seventh century. Wahhabis and other militant Muslims wish to usher in a new age of Islamic dominance where Islam can again advance undeterred.

With the defeat of the colonialist nations, the independence of Muslim states, and the vulnerability of much of the West, militant Muslim imams around the world are sounding the trumpet that a new "Golden Age" of Islam is approaching. If that is the case, it obviously will not bode well for poets or polytheists, Jews or journalists. For if Muslims follow the path of their prophet, no ethic is absolute, no treaty secure. The words of Winston Churchill from the year 1899 prove prophetic:

> Individual Moslems may show splendid qualities. Thousands become the brave and loyal soldiers of the Queen; all know how to die; but the influence of the religion paralyses the social development of those who follow it. No stronger retrograde force exists in the world. Far from being moribund, Mohammedanism is a militant and proselytizing faith. It has already spread throughout Central Africa, raising fearless warriors at every step; and were it not that Christianity is sheltered in the strong arms of science, the science against which it had vainly struggled, the civilization of modern Europe might fall, as fell the civilization of ancient Rome.[14]

More than a century ago, Churchill's foresight was as keen as his military genius. It was Churchill, the brilliant politician and military historian, who understood Muhammad, himself a brutal yet brilliant politician and warrior, better than any Westerner in modern times.

Jihad As Carried Forward by Muhammad's Early Successors

Remember that if you suffer a few moments in patience, you will afterward enjoy supreme delight. Do not imagine that your fate can be separated from mine, and rest assured that if you fall, I shall perish with you, or avenge you. You have heard that in this country there are a large number of ravishingly beautiful Greek maidens, their graceful forms are draped in sumptuous gowns on which gleam pearls, coral, and purest gold, and they live in the palaces of royal kings.

The Commander of True Believers, Alwalid, son of Abdalmelik, has chosen you for this attack from among all his Arab warriors; and he promises that you shall become his comrades and shall hold the rank of kings in this country. Such is his confidence in your intrepidity. The one fruit which he desires to obtain from your bravery is that the word of God shall be exalted in this country, and that the true religion shall be established here. The spoils will belong to yourselves. [1]

—TARIQ IBN ZIYAD

The above scene seems all too familiar: A Muslim jihadist declares war on the infidels of Europe, declaring that the land needs to exalt the "true religion" and that all material possessions will belong to the victorious Muslims. As Allah wills, many will die a glorious death. But they will be freed from the pains of this life and enjoy the "supreme delight" of Paradise, including the "ravishingly beautiful maidens" that await every martyr. A quintessential Muslim declaration of war, this address recognizes the superficial superiority of the enemy—as Tariq adds, "[The land is] protected by an innumerable army; he has men in abundance, but you, as your only aid, have your own swords"[2]—but victory is promised, because Allah is on the side of the Muslim.

This address, although typical of today's jihadists, was actually given at the turn of the eighth century. This was a time when Muslim holy warriors went practically unopposed in their conquest of the Middle East, North Africa, and finally Europe. By 711, Islamic leaders were confident that, in the same way much of the world had already submitted, so too would Europe bow its Christian knee to the "true religion." The Zoroastrians were defeated in Persia, the Byzantine Christians were humiliated in Egypt, and now the Roman Christians and the Jews were to be crushed in the heartland of Western Christianity. Within a few months, inhabitants of the Iberian Peninsula, which today comprises Spain and Portugal, surrendered to Islamic forces. It seemed it was only a matter of time before the entirety of the civilized world would yield to Islam.

> Contemporary Islam... hopes that a return to Islamic traditionalism will usher in a new age of Islamic supremacy.

When we consider the motivations of twenty-first-century jihadists, we must first look back to these years, the formative years of holy war after Muhammad's death. There, we see the hopes and dreams that were unfulfilled by the prophet now carried out by his successors. We see not only why jihad was to be undertaken, but how it was accomplished.

The horrendous slaughter and brutal aftermath of Islamic conquest became notorious throughout much of the world. Islam's desire to subjugate the world to itself was evident to all nations that surrounded the new global force. And finally, the conquest was not only one of political-military force, but of religious persuasion as well. What Islam viewed as false faiths were eradicated or subjugated. Many of them, like their adherents, did not survive as lands were cleansed from religious perversions.

It is crucial to understand that much of the inspiration and many of today's tactics for jihad find their origins within the first few generations of Islamic history. Although every religion has its manifestations of violence, Islam was violent from its inception. Though Christianity has been wickedly brutal during much of its history, it did not claim political and religious conquest until it became unified with the Roman government. From its beginning, however, Islam was on the offensive, aggressively targeting infidel nations and passionately desiring global domination. Consider this one fact when comparing early Islam with early Christianity: *The disciples of Christ, with the exception of the apostle John, all died for the faith. The disciples of Muhammad, with no major exceptions, all killed for the faith.*

Contemporary Islam, much of which desires to purify itself and mirror early Islam, hopes that a return to Islamic traditionalism will usher in a new age of Islamic supremacy. Here, many modern Muslims hope to finish what Tariq ibn Ziyad began: the Islamization of Europe.[3]

15

How did those who knew Muhammad understand jihad?

Subsequent to Muhammad's death, the leaders of Islam swiftly prevailed over major cities and territories, including the following:[4]

- Damascus, Syria (634–635)

- Antioch, Syria (636)

- Ctesiphon, capital of the Persian Empire (637), near which Baghdad was founded (762)

- Jerusalem, Israel (638)

- Alexandria, Egypt (641)

- Hamadan, final conquest of the Persian Empire (642)

- Cyprus (649)

By 650, Muslims, once a small minority within the Arabian Peninsula, had reached the Atlantic Ocean and were setting their sights on

Europe. The territories of the southern Caucasus—Georgia, Armenia, and Azerbaijan—were also in the hands of Muslim rulers.

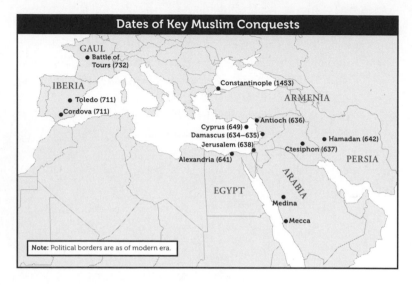

Dates of Key Muslim Conquests

GAUL
● Battle of Tours (732)

IBERIA

Constantinople (1453)

ARMENIA

● Toledo (711)
● Cordova (711)

● Antioch (636)

Cyprus (649) ●
Damascus (634–635) ●
Jerusalem (638) ●

● Hamadan (642)

Ctesiphon (637)

PERSIA

Alexandria (641)

EGYPT

ARABIA

● Medina

● Mecca

Note: Political borders are as of modern era.

The majority of these cities and territories that suffered the wrath of Muslim warriors had been ruled by Orthodox Christians[5] For example, citizens of Alexandria watched in terror as their enemy "destroyed its walls, and burnt many churches with fire."[6]

Once Islam was established and Christians were subdued and humiliated, discussions began on the fate of non-Muslims and their structures. Umar, the second leader of Islam, argued that minorities and their structures, once surrendered, are protected as long as they abide by Islamic rule. He declared, "Nor shall injury be done to them or to their compounds, or to their crosses, nor shall their properties be injured in any way."[7] But contemporaries of Umar such as Ibn Taymiyyah documented the limitations to these sympathies,[8] such as:

- Christians have no right to build new places of worship.
- Christians have no right to remodel a church in conquered lands.

- Muslims could confiscate places of worship in towns taken by storm.

- Muslims could destroy every church in conquered lands.

Additionally, the surrender treaty—now commonly known as the Pact of Umar (explained on page 10)—went against the very character of Christianity as expressed in the Great Commission (Matthew 28:18-20). Christians were forbidden to share their faith and had to choose whether they would follow Muhammad's regulations or Christ's command. As for those who disregarded the surrender treaty, Umar decreed,

> Anyone who violates such terms will be unprotected. And it will be permissible for the Muslims to treat them as rebels or dissenters namely, it is permissible to kill them.[9]

16

Brother on brother: How did Muslims view other Muslims?

> *O People, listen to me in earnest, worship ALLAH, say your five daily prayers (Salah), fast during the month of Ramadhan, and give your wealth in Zakat. Perform Hajj if you can afford to. You know that every Muslim is the brother of another Muslim. You are all equal. Nobody has superiority over other except by piety and good action.*[10]

—MUHAMMAD'S FINAL SERMON BEFORE DEATH

Islamic expansion seemed unstoppable. But increasing internal strife, a significant problem from the early days of Islam, interrupted the crusade toward global ascendancy. Three of the first four leaders of Islam were killed by those they trusted most. Umar, the second caliph (634–644) was stabbed by a Persian slave. The third caliph, Uthman (644–656) was struck in the head while reading the Qur'an. Ali, the fourth caliph (656–661) was assassinated by disgruntled Muslims while praying at a mosque.

Muslim infighting and civil war are as old as Islam itself. From the beginning, they have involved not just the leaders, but entire groups and peoples. When Abu Bakr took the mantle from Muhammad, he immediately had to deal with rebellion in the Arabian Peninsula. The people of Yamama, a district east of Mecca and Medina, had agreed to an allegiance with Muhammad that, they argued, ended upon his death. A Muslim army was sent to crush the rebellion and bring these pagans back into submission to Islam. They needed a lesson: once a Muslim territory, always a Muslim territory.

Near the beginning of the reign of Ali, Muhammad's youngest wife, Aisha, revolted against the caliph for his refusal to seek out and punish Uthman's assassin. Thus, within 25 years of Muhammad's death, Muslim was fighting Muslim. The major battle of this rebellion, known as the Battle of the Camel (656), witnessed the defeat of Aisha, who was escorted back to Medina to live in seclusion until her death in 678. And 10,000 Muslims lay dead. The damage was far-reaching, and it opened wounds that remain to the present day. Islam split into two paths: those who supported Ali, the *Shia;* and the vast majority who accepted the traditional leadership, the *Sunni.*

The enmity between the two parties boiled over in the year 680. Caliph Yazid I was pitted against Husayn, the grandson of Muhammad and son of Ali. Husayn refused to submit himself to Yazid's rule and instead instituted "true Islam" under his own leadership. Yazid, of course, swiftly responded to the rebellion. He routed the Shiite opposition at the Battle of Karbala in what is now southern Iraq.

Yazid's forces beheaded Husayn and slaughtered his family. All men in Husayn's forces were immediately killed, while women and children were taken into custody. The prisoners were forced to travel across much of Iraq on foot or camel, which caused many to perish along the way. In essence, fellow Muslims were treated like infidels. Today, Shiite Muslims commemorate the martyrdom of Husayn on the Day of Ashura, when they reenact the valiant struggle of their hero and his comrades on that fateful day.

17

Continuing conquest: How was
Islam introduced into Europe?

Once the infidel Muslims—defined as those who rebelled against recognized authority—were put in their place, Islam was once more free to expand with few hindrances. Muslims entered the Iberian Peninsula in the first years of the eighth century and claimed victory in the major cities of Cordova and Toledo by the end of 711 (see map on page 44). Within a few more years, the entirety of the peninsula, with the exception of the northwest section, was lost to the Christian Visigoths and ruled by the Arab Muslims.[11]

The Muslims were ready to move farther—into Gaul (now France), one of the major centers of Roman Christianity. And who was going to stop them anyway? Muslims were virtually undefeated in battle. For some ten years they continued to advance against foes who, like the Visigoths, were in political disarray. But the Franks, under the leadership of Charles Martel, marshaled their forces together near the towns of Poitiers and Tours and, in 732, defeated the Islamic forces. One chronicle, although written with proud and prejudiced exaggeration, indicates the significance of the victory:

> The Muslims planned to go to Tours to destroy the Church of St. Martin, the city, and the whole country. Then came against them the glorious Prince Charles, at the head of his whole force. He drew up his host, and he fought as fiercely as the hungry wolf falls upon the stag. By the grace of Our Lord, he wrought a great slaughter upon the enemies of Christian faith, so that—as history bears witness—he slew in that battle 300,000 men, likewise their king by name Abderrahman. Then was he [Charles] first called "Martel," for as a hammer of iron, of steel, and of every other metal, even so he dashed: and smote in the battle all his enemies.[12]

Muslims, including their ruler Abd al-Rahman, were killed by the thousands. In Islamic theology, it appeared that Allah's wrath had fallen on Muslims, because infidels had defeated the chosen of Allah. The day of prosperity had ended, and the day of judgment had begun. The Muslims were forced to retreat and analyze the demoralizing defeat. Eventually they would again attack Christianity, but the next time their attempts would be from the east.

Some historians now relegate the Battle of Tours to the everyday skirmishes of military history. But considering the issues in this section of our book and today's current events, it seems clear that the Franks' victory halted the onslaught of the Islamic empire.

Further, the victory allowed the Franks to gain power and then unify much of Western Europe under the leadership of Charles Martel's grandson, Charlemagne. On Christmas Day 800, Charlemagne was crowned emperor of the Holy Roman Empire by Pope Leo III.[13] Here the once divided Europe began its rise to prominence—and to political and religious power that would endure for more than a millennium. Europe would quickly cast its own version of theocracy, built on the Roman Catholic system of hierarchical rule by the pope, which would lead to the persecution of millions of Jews, Eastern Christians, and free-church Christians.[14]

Perhaps it will be a twenty-first-century jihad that will cause a divided West to unify around the modern—not medieval—tenets it so deeply cherishes. Democracy and liberty, often taken for granted in much of the West, will then perhaps find a firm place in the hearts and minds of its people.

Jihad from Islam's Greatest Years to the Present

The figure of Sayyid Qutb serves as a twentieth-century example of how one person can reshape the global politics of Islam and the way it carries out jihad. In November 1948, Qutb (1906 1966), then an official in the Egyptian Ministry of Education, was sent to the United States to study the American schooling system.

He was assigned to Greeley, Colorado, home of the University of Northern Colorado. There, his presuppositions and previous life experience caused him to view the United States as repugnant and decadent. About women, he concluded,

> The American girl is well acquainted with her body's seductive capacity. She knows it lies in the face, and in expressive eyes, and thirsty lips. She knows seductiveness lies in the round breasts, the full buttocks, and in the shapely thighs, sleek legs—and she shows all this and does not hide it.[1]

Needless to say, his view was based entirely on his experience of Islamic women, and thus it was more perception than reality. Indeed, Greeley, Colorado, was a staunchly conservative town with a strong religious base. It was a planned community that even forbade the consumption of alcohol.[2]

By the time of his return to Egypt in 1950, Qutb, already critical of Western values, was solid in his belief that the West was immersed in paganism and a "culture of greed." Only Islamic law (*sharia*), based on the entire community (*umma*), was the right path for the governments of the world.

An Egyptian Muslim looks at religion in America

Sayyid Qutb even recorded his view of the modern American church. Bernard Lewis summarizes Qutb's perceptions:

> Churches in America, he said, operate like businesses, competing for clients and publicity, and using the same methods as stores and theaters to attract customers and audiences. For the minister of the church, as for the manager of a business or of a theater, success is what matters, and success is measured by size—bigness, numbers. To attract clientele, churches advertise shamelessly and offer what American's most seek—"a good time" or "fun."[3]

Qutb's views became so polarizing that he was forced to resign his post in the Egyptian government. Shortly thereafter, he joined the Muslim Brotherhood, an organization that worked for the imposition of sharia law and traditional Islamic social structure.

Qutb's radical proclamations eventually found their way into mainstream Islamic thought. He believed that the West, shot through with the infidel mind-set, had won over much of the Muslim community. For this reason, he insisted, much of Muslim society was in a new "age of ignorance" (*jahiliyya*). Historically, this age was defined as the "period of paganism that prevailed in Arabia before the advent of the Prophet and of Islam."[4]

Thus, in Qutb's thought, there was 1) an external enemy—the West and its support for secularism and Zionism; and 2) an internal enemy—those Muslim elements that had succumbed to the West, thus allying themselves with the external enemy and its values. Both seductresses, he proclaimed, must be silenced. In the end, the Egyptian government silenced Qutb by hanging, for plotting the assassination of Egypt's president. But his works and worldview still live on in much of the Islamic world today. He is, in a strong sense, the poster child for modern Islamic jihad.

Throughout Islamic history, crucial people, such as Qutb, and crucial events have shaped the politics of succeeding generations. These events do not simply define a generation; they define a movement, a religion. In Islamic warfare, five events previous to Sayyid Qutb's time deserve attention because they illustrate the Islamic view of jihad for those ages, as well as the general view that holds sway into our day.

18

The rise of Baghdad: Was the "Golden Age" of Islam that golden?

After Muslims suffered humiliating defeat at the hands of Charles Martel and the Franks, the ruling party of Islam, the Umayyad dynasty (centered in Damascus), collapsed and was replaced by the Abbasids. They would renew Islamic dominance and move the capital of Islam to Baghdad (762).[5] This shift in power ushered in what is known as the "Golden Age of Islam," a period that would last from the eighth century into the thirteenth century.

This period was energized by one of the military heroes of Islamic history, Harun al-Rashid (763–809), who repeatedly defeated Byzantine Christian forces in Asia Minor and required them to pay heavy tribute to the Abbasid dynasty on an annual basis. As al-Rashid enriched his treasury through Islamic aggression, Baghdad began to thrive in wealth and prosperity. Cultural advancements in areas including philosophy, mathematics, art, and science were pronounced. One author comments,

> What an exciting time it was! Students from Europe and from the far corners of the empire flocked to Islamic universities. Mathematicians introduced what we know as Arabic numerals and set out the principles of algebra. Physicians identified the causes and treatment of smallpox and other diseases and wrote the textbooks that would be used in Europe until well into the sixteenth century. From great observatories astronomers measured the earth and mapped the heavens.[6]

It seemed that Islam was a safe haven for intellectual stimulation and a bulwark for scientific advances.

Yet, while advances were being made in many areas of learning, classical Islamic scholars recognize this era as the "Golden Age" not merely due to intellectual achievements, but more because of the strong implementation of *sharia* (Islamic law). The rise of learning and education also gave rise to the *Hadiths* (reports, or stories), collections of the sayings and works of Muhammad to which strict adherence was required (sura 33:21). The two most respected (*sahih*) collections were compiled during the height of the Golden Age by two Islamic scholars, Muhammad al-Bukhari (810–870) and Abul Husayn Muslim (821–875). These collections meticulously outlined the acceptable (*halal*) and forbidden (*haram*) practices for the everyday Muslim in areas as minute as menstruation and nutrition and as significant as jihad, taxes, and religious exercises. Any noncompliance was to be met with severe punishment, as also detailed in these collections.

Thus Muhammad's life, words, and actions were permanently codified and displayed in written form, ever to be enforced by Islamic courts. The Golden Age of Islam was thus the formative stage of oppression and persecution. The Hadith provided the requisite authority to impose laws regarding food, taxes, and dress. Islam, hailed as the supreme faith, meted out punishment to thieves (Bukhari 8.780: "cutting off of hands"), adulterers (Bukhari 2.413: "stoning"), and apostates (Bukhari 9.57: "kill him"),[7] as well as 80 lashes for imbibers of alcoholic beverages (Muslim 17.4226).

Moreover, these collections set in stone the meaning and purpose of jihad. As mentioned earlier, Bukhari dedicated an entire book (book 52, "Jihad") of his compilation to the subject of war. Muslim's Hadith followed suit in a section entitled "The Book of Jihad and Expedition" (book 19). As seen in this collection, the life and commands of Muhammad articulated the offensive strategy Muslims were to undertake in making Islam universal (Muslim 19.4311):

- Muslims were to aggressively confront all enemies of Islam (19.4315) and know that they would be given victory. Allah would not allow defeat since there would be "none on earth to worship Thee" (19.4318).

- The killing of women was permissible in some circumstances as long as it was unintentional (19.4321), and the environment could be ravaged "to disgrace the evil-doers" (19.4324).

- The spoils of war were the property of the Muslim victors (19.4327).

- Jews and Christians were to be expelled from lands, including the Arabian Peninsula (19.4366), and were not to be trusted as allies (19.4472).

Viewed through the lens of history, the greatest "advancement" of the Golden Age was the definition and pursuit of jihad.

19

The recapture of Jerusalem: Does Islam advocate removal of the Jews?

In October 1187, Saladin, considered one of the most valiant war heroes in the history of Islam, recaptured Jerusalem from Christian crusaders after besieging it for a few weeks. A history article describes the events:

> The Muslim general captured the holy city. Muslims immediately clambered up and removed the cross that the Crusaders had mounted on the cupola of the Dome of the Rock. According to an eyewitness, the combined roar of the Muslims shouting "Allah is greatest!" and the groans of the defeated Crusaders, watching the fall of their sacred symbol, were so loud they shook the ground.[8]

This episode demonstrates the crusader view so deeply ingrained in Islamic warfare (although Saladin treated his captives far more graciously

...f his Christian contemporaries treated Muslim prisoners[9]).
...arfare is profoundly religious in nature and scope, and vic-
...Christians meant re-establishing Muslim dominance over
the subdued region. Jewish scholar Bat Ye'or describes the persecution
that was reinstated by Saladin:

> In Egypt, Syria, and Palestine, Saladin (1169–1193) revived the
> Covenant of Umar. Persecutions of Jews and especially Chris-
> tians increased during the rule of the Mamluks (1250–1517).
> Under the influence of the *ulama* [Muslim scholars], dis-
> crimination, humiliation, massacres, fiscal extortions, forced
> conversions, and the destruction of churches and synagogues
> occurred.[10]

In Jerusalem, Saladin re-established not only Islamic dominance, but
also Islamic law. The same rules that were applied to early victims of
jihad in the seventh century were reinstituted in the twelfth century.

The significance of Jerusalem to Islam. Jerusalem is especially cher-
ished by Muslims since they believe Allah gave them the land through
Abraham's oldest son, Ishmael. Muhammad revised the biblical story of
Ishmael (recognized as a "wild man"—Genesis 16:12—but nonetheless
a Jew) to make him the promised son of Abraham and Hagar. Indeed,
Muslims generally agree that it was Ishmael who was to be sacrificed
(sura 37:99-107), although the Qur'an is not explicit in the matter. They
believe it was Abraham—who, according to the Qur'an was neither a
Jew nor Christian (sura 3:67), but a Muslim (sura 2:135)—who permanently and perpetually bequeathed the land to Ishmael. Incredibly,
Jerusalem remained in the hands of Muslims from the time of Saladin
until the end of World War I.

Since 1917, when British forces defeated the Ottoman Turks and
captured the holy city, Jerusalem has been controlled by infidels—first
Christians (1917–1948) and then Jews (1948–present). This is wholly
unacceptable in the traditional Muslim worldview, which believes that
Muslims inherited the land theologically (as described above) and captured the land historically through Umar (in 638) and Saladin.

Thus, in Islamic thinking, the land belongs to the Muslim and must be recaptured. Jews are to be treated in the same way they were treated in the Arabian Peninsula during the time of Muhammad and his early successors—driven out or killed. Ye'or explains:

> The fate of Jews in Arabia was conceived as the prototype by later legislators and jurists in their relations with other nations... On the other hand, the Muslim government who rejects the ideology of *jihad* might establish relations with Israel within a context of the legitimacy of the sovereign rights of nations.[11]

Conversion, expulsion, or worse. History is the window that allows a twenty-first-century observer to peer in and see how the words of Muhammad have caused the slaughter of millions of Jews. They are considered "fools" (1.392) who cannot be trusted (sura 5:51). They are cursed by Allah (sura 4:46; Bukhari 2.414), perpetual enemies of Allah (sura 4:160), and warmongers "who strive to make mischief in the land" (sura 5:64). One tradition communicates the words of Muhammad himself:

> It has been narrated on the authority of Abu Huraira who said: We were (sitting) in the mosque when the Messenger of Allah (may peace be upon him) came to us and said: (Let us) go to the Jews. We went out with him until we came to them. The Messenger of Allah (may peace be upon him) stood up and called out to them (saying): O ye assembly of Jews, accept Islam (and) you will be safe. They said: Abu'l-Qasim, you have communicated (God's Message to us). The Messenger of Allah (may peace be upon him) said: I want this (i.e. you should admit that God's Message has been communicated to you), accept Islam and you would be safe. They said: Abu'l-Qisim, you have communicated (Allah's Message). The Messenger of Allah (may peace be upon him) said: I want this...
>
> He said to them (the same words) the third time (and on getting the same reply) he added: You should know that the earth belongs to Allah and His Apostle, and I wish that I

should expel you from this land. Those of you who have any property with them should sell it, otherwise they should know that the *earth belongs to Allah* and His Apostle (and they may have to go away leaving everything behind).[12]

Muhammad, according to the greatest source of Islamic authority outside the Qur'an, targeted Jews and demanded they convert or be banished. The incontrovertible conclusion is quite plain in the above quote: Islam believes not only that Jerusalem is their Promised Land, but also that the whole "earth belongs to Allah." Consequently, non-Jews will be treated in similar fashion to the Jews of the past.

20

Constantinople and the end of Eastern Orthodox rule: How does jihad affect Christian churches?

Perhaps the best example of jihad's goal of political imperialism came when Ottoman Turkish forces overran Constantinople in 1453. That great city was the epicenter of Eastern Christianity and the seat of its patriarch, Athanasius II[13]; it was ruled by the Byzantine emperor Constantine XI.

> "He dismounted in front of the cathedral… and proclaimed the *shahadah*: 'There is no god but Allah, and Muhammad is His prophet.'"

Located at the very point that Europe meets Asia, the city was strategically highly desirable. Over time, numerous adversaries, including Avars (Mongols), Persians, Arabs, Bulgarians, and Russians, attempted to conquer the mighty city, all to no avail. The only opponent able to effectively defeat the Byzantines, and that only for a short while, was the Roman Catholic crusaders who sacked the city at the beginning of the thirteenth century. Nonetheless, the constant onslaught by rivals weakened the city and reduced the Byzantines' territory so that by the turn of the fifteenth century, the emperor's subjects numbered only about 50,000.[14]

Like his father before him, the Ottoman sultan Mehmet II (1432–1481) gathered his forces in hope of conquering the seemingly invincible metropolis. In May 1453, he declared jihad, promising his troops that Muhammad's prophecy—that Constantinople would be ruled by Muslims—would come true.[15] The results were brutal:

> On 29 May 1453 his army made the blood flow like rain after a storm, and corpses float to the sea like melons on a canal, according to one observer, Nicolo Barbaro. The last Byzantine Emperor, Constantine XI, fought to the end of his life and his empire. Some 30,000 Christians were either enslaved or sold. Sultan Mehmet rode on a white horse towards the cathedral of Hagia Sophia, mother of all churches, built in the sixth century by Justinian. He dismounted in front of the cathedral, picked up a handful of dust, poured it over his turban and proclaimed the *shahadah:* "There is no god but Allah, and Muhammad is His prophet." The cathedral in that instant became a mosque.[16]

Whereas the early Muslims built the Dome of the Rock upon the site of the old Jewish temple in Jerusalem in 691, the Ottoman Muslims demonstrated Islamic superiority not through destruction but through occupation. Constantinople, renamed Istanbul, emerged as the center of Islam. As the gateway to Europe, it allowed Ottoman forces to set their sights on that continent, beginning with the Balkans and eventually moving as far west as Vienna (which was besieged in 1520 and 1683). A new empire, the Ottoman Empire, had ascended to dominate part of the globe, founded on the old Islamic principle of holy war. Jihad was alive and well.

21

The rulers of Saudi Arabia: Are the Wahhabis extremists or traditionalists?

Although the Ottoman Empire expanded and thrived in much of the Eurasian world, including North Africa and the Middle East, the acceleration of Western colonialism in the eighteenth century halted Islamic expansion and diminished the House of Islam. The defeat of the Turks at Vienna in 1683 cleared the way for European dominance over the next two-and-a-half centuries. Ottoman strongholds fell into the hands of infidel Europeans. Over this period, part of the Balkans was ceded to Austria, Algeria came under French rule, and much of east Africa was governed by Great Britain.

Even territories gained during the first three centuries of Islam were now under the rule of the infidels. Great Britain possessed India and modern-day Pakistan as part of its empire. Russia, dominating the Ottomans during the nineteenth-century Russo-Turkish Wars, advanced in traditionally Muslim strongholds in Central Asia. After World War I, Persia was divided by the Russians and the British.

In 1924, the final blow of devastation occurred when Mustafa Atatürk, president of the newly formed Republic of Turkey, secularized the Turkish government and dismantled the Islamic Caliphate (discussed in more detail on pages 19–20). The caliphate, the great leadership council of Islam that had presided over the major affairs of Islam since the time of Muhammad, no longer existed. Traditional Islam entered the lowest ebb of its history.

At the very point that Islam was shaken to its core, the modern Saudi nation gained independence. In 1932, after the House of Saud had unified the major cities and holy sites of the Arabian Peninsula under its rule, the royal family declared the united territories as the Kingdom of Saudi Arabia.

An absolute monarchy, Saudi Arabia advanced quickly due to its massive oil reserves, the largest of any nation in the world. And perhaps most crucial to world affairs, the religious aspects of the kingdom, which included the two holiest sites in Islam, were guided by Wahhabi-trained jurists and scholars. Wahhabism, named after its founder Muhammad ibn Abd al-Wahhab (1703–1792), advocated a strict and literal interpretation of the Qur'an and the Hadith. It rejected evolved doctrines of Islam, such as the practice of using a prophet's name during prayer and the visitation of the graves of saints, both practiced in Shia Islam.

The basis of reform determines its outcome

Though Wahhabism is portrayed as an extreme form of Islam by much of the Western media (and by some Muslims), it is actually a reform movement somewhat similar to the Protestant Reformation. It desired to return to the original sources of the faith. It affirmed the literal interpretation of its sacred text and rejected the newer innovations of tradition and custom.

But at this point the comparison fails. The enormous difference between the two movements is not in their intentions, but in their sources. When one takes a literal interpretation of the Bible and follows the life of Christ, one becomes more peaceful (Matthew 5:8-10); when one takes a literal interpretation of the Qur'an and follows the example of Muhammad, one becomes more militant (sura 8:12). When educators or media sources argue that Islam is in dire need of a reformation, they truly demonstrate their ignorance—since today's situation is the *outcome* of a true (and perhaps radical) Islamic reformation.

From this, it is clear that Wahhabism is not an extreme form of Islam. It is a purist form, which finds its justification in Islam and early Islamic history.[17] If we keep this in mind, we can understand that Saudi Arabia's lack of religious liberty and human rights—as well as its demand for strict conformity to dress and customs within the Islamic community—is a grave reminder of what Islam was like in the seventh century. Moreover, the Wahhabi declaration of other Muslims as heretics, a declaration unwelcome to much of the Muslim community, recalls the early conflicts among Muslims and the battle over the soul of Islam. As well, the denigration of women, the hostility toward other faiths, and the elevation of religious authority are all reminiscent of the days of Muhammad.

It is critical to realize that Wahhabism is a major force driving much of Islam today. It is responsible for building thousands of mosques around the world, opening hundreds of Islamic schools (*madrassas*) all over the globe, and funding or owning many of the media outlets most popular among Muslims.

The struggle for the soul of Islam is now amplified as Wahhabi scholars pit themselves against other Sunni scholars. The re-emergence of traditional Islam, along with some traits that are radical, casts a dark cloud over the future of a more temperate Islam, such as that displayed in the Turkish Republic. It seems clear that the day of the Turkish experiment with democracy is waning; the day of Saudi totalitarianism is at hand.

C

What the future holds depends upon who emerges as the leading voice of Islam. If the Islamic leadership council, the caliphate, is ever revived, Islam will once again unify itself around a common unbelieving enemy. At that point, many assume that a new Cold War will be launched.

But that is not necessarily the case. The Cold War centered on an ideology which could be struck down fairly easily. However, this new war—perhaps we can call it the Confessional War—is founded upon theology, one for which millions are willing to die. A new Cold War will not emerge, but a new Crusade may. The likelihood that such a war would last for centuries is nearly certain.

Our Response to Jihad

The era in which we live, which could be termed the Age of Cynicism, is fraught with such characteristics as the polarization of groups that have different agendas and worldviews. Adding a level of contentiousness, many observers of our era have formed a highly critical view of this highly critical generation, which only makes the situation worse.

While the skepticism of our day can be cause for concern, history records the benefits of such times. In fact, each era's low point has given people of that period an opportunity to honestly analyze their troubles and tumult— and this analysis has, in turn, often led to some kind of resurgence.

For example, the growing irreligiosity of America in the early 1700s prompted men such as Jonathan Edwards to give a clarion call for repentance. The result was the beginning of the first Great Awakening. The Great Awakening did not unify all Christians in America, but it did identify who these Christians were. Some of them scoffed or balked at the movement and rejected it outright. Others embraced the offer of renewal and made a new beginning of religious conviction that would impact generations to come for Christ.

Likewise, Muslims and Christians have been greatly divided in previous times. The most prominent display of this divide was unquestionably the Crusades (1095–1291). The endless bloodshed and atrocities on both sides caused a separation that still remains. Nonetheless, the low point of the Crusades also brought some positive outcomes, not the least of which was the exchange of knowledge and ideas between the two sides. Muslims shared their advances in art, medicine, philosophy, and the sciences—and these, in many ways, were responsible for encouraging the Renaissance and, later, the Reformation. Christians shared their wealth, commerce, philosophy, and political theory.

In the twenty-first century, this exchange of ideas has now come full circle, and new discussions and debates have emerged. In America, where the last two generations have largely remained illiterate in the area of religion, many people are now realizing the importance of religion in any historical or cultural conversation.

But a word to all: *For these discussions and debates to be truly beneficial, they must be adamantly honest.* "Political correctness," if welcomed and allowed to take over, will devastate any candid exchange between the sincere proponents of the two religious systems. Truth, not diversity of thought, must be the ultimate goal.

In pursuit of that aim, this final section will speak first to Christians, then to Muslims who are reading this work.

22

To the Christian: Do you have an appreciation for your faith?

When first introduced to Islam in its most devout form, a person can be awestruck by the full surrender of many Muslims around the world. Observe the millions of devout followers who earnestly respond to the call to prayer five times a day and gather together at their local mosque. Observe the multitudes who dedicate themselves to the fast for one lunar month of each year, abstaining from food, drink, and other pleasures. Observe the three million Muslims who annually make their way to the holiest city in Islam, Mecca, and unite themselves in prayer around the Kaaba as well as visiting the site of Muhammad's last sermon and throwing stones at the devil.

Additionally, tens of thousands of Muslims worldwide have memorized all 114 chapters of the Qur'an in Arabic and can recite it on command. Islam is a cradle-to-the-grave religion that calls for surrender, complete surrender, which can be easily seen by a Muslim's actions, dress, and demeanor.

But do not stop at the surface of Islam. Look deeper and you will recognize that these actions are intense attempts by Muslims to appease Allah, in hope that he will one day allow them into Paradise. Adherents of Islam always bear these heavy weights:

- No hope is certain (Muslim 37.6638), even for Muhammad (Bukhari 5.266), and it is Allah's prerogative to do whatever he wishes (sura 14:4).

- Upon the foundation of repentance and faith, works are imperative for any Muslim who even hopes he can enter Paradise (sura 25:70).

- Responsibility is "fastened to your own neck" (sura 17:13), and your good works and bad works will one day be balanced on the scales of judgment (sura 23:101-103).

- The love Allah shows to humans is conditional, based upon good works (sura 2:190); grave sins will definitely lead to "the Fire."*

Even when fully aware of Islam's own system of guidance, few can achieve the demands of the faith. If a Muslim does not practice alms-giving, he will not enter heaven (Bukhari 2.498). If a Muslim commits suicide, he will enter the flames of hell (Bukhari 2.446). Indeed, infants who die before birth, even though they would have been born "upright" (sura 30:29-30), will enter hell (Muslim 33.6435). Is it any wonder that Muslims so willingly go to their deaths in jihad—when it is the only act that, by the promise of the Qur'an, can secure heaven for the individual (sura 3:157)?

By considering these crushing religious burdens, many of today's Christians can gain a far greater appreciation for the salvation God has given to us. Consider the following:

---

* See, among many other examples, suras 2:217; 4:145; 10:027; 52:11-13.

- God loved the world unconditionally (Romans 5:8; 2 Peter 3:9); Christ died in our place (Galatians 2:20) so that we would have eternal life (John 3:16).

- This promise has no conditions to it since God transforms those who believe in Christ from the inside out (2 Corinthians 5:17) and will certainly complete his work in his time (Philippians 1:6).

- Because Christ came in the form of a slave and humbled himself (Philippians 2:5-11), we are therefore to taste "the fellowship of His sufferings" and be "conformed to His death" (Philippians 3:10 NASB).

Our lives must be fully surrendered to Christ, not to earn salvation, but as an expression of thanks to God for providing our salvation. Anything less is a mockery of Christ's life, death, and resurrection. Our call is not to *live*, but to *life*. For that to be the case, we must first die to self. Remember, a faith worth living for is a faith worth dying for. And a faith worth dying for will be a faith worth living for.

23

To the Muslim: Are you willing to seek and surrender?

No one knows the faith described above more thoroughly than a former Muslim living in a Muslim-dominated country. When a Muslim man or woman confesses their faith in the Lord Jesus Christ as their God and Savior, thereby becoming an infidel, persecution follows without regard to their welfare. "Mild" persecution includes the loss of one's job and, most likely, the loss of part or all of one's family. Men may be imprisoned, while women are "re-educated" in the Islamic faith. Severe persecution includes beatings, exile, and death, usually by beheading.

Yet ask a former Muslim if their decision is worth the pain, and you will hear the words of someone with no regrets. They have been set free by the power of Christ, something that cannot be taken away from them. They now have a relationship with the Creator of this world, and he speaks to them through his Word, the Bible.

Like millions before them, they have gladly surrendered everything. They did not come into the Christian faith blind. The Lord himself promised persecution (Matthew 10:33-34). The apostles were prime examples of suffering the onslaught of persecution (Acts 7:54-60), and they acknowledged it as the very will of God (Philippians 1:21). The offer is there for you to accept or reject. Would you be willing to lose everything in order to "gain Christ" (Philippians 3:8)?

We know that many doubts about Christianity must be in your mind. Ultimately, the question of which is true comes down to which revelation you trust. There are only three options:[1]

1. The Qur'an is the Word of Allah;

2. The Bible is the Word of God;

3. Neither of the two is a revelation from God.

Of course, both texts give internal evidence that they are inspired by God Almighty. The Qur'an asserts that it is irreproducible (sura 2:23), incorruptible (sura 15:9), and superior to previous revelations (sura 5:15). It calls itself a "tablet preserved" (sura 85:22). It is supposed to be a "guide and a mercy to those who believe"* (sura 16:64).

> Here are a few questions you as a Muslim may wish to ask yourself...

The Bible, for its part, declares that it is fully inspired (2 Timothy 3:16) in its very words (Matthew 5:17-18) and was written that "you may believe that Jesus is the Christ, the Son of God; and that believing you may have life in His name" (John 20:31 NASB). Indeed, even the Qur'an acknowledges that portions of the Bible were inspired, including the Torah, the Psalms of David, and the Gospel (sura 3:2-3).

A question must then be raised: If the Torah was inspired by Allah

---

* From Abdullah Yusuf Ali, tr., *The Holy Quran.*

and then lost or corrupted; if the Psalms of David were inspired by Allah and then lost or corrupted; and if the Gospel was inspired by Allah and then lost or corrupted—why would you trust Allah to preserve his word the fourth time (that is, the Qur'an) when he did not or was not able to do so the first three times?

Moreover, because of its content, further questions are raised about the veracity of the Qur'an. It is a repudiation of the Bible in very many ways, perhaps the most notable in the subject of Christ's death. The Qur'an denies the crucifixion of Christ (sura 4:157-158), teaching that it was "Someone likened unto him."*

Of course, the entirety of the Christian faith is based on the death and subsequent resurrection of Christ (1 Corinthians 15). Which is true? It is obvious that the Bible proclaims Christ's death on the cross numerous times (Matthew 26; Mark 14; Luke 22; John 19). Central tenets of the Christian faith, including baptism and the Lord's Supper, are based on Christ's death (and resurrection). Here are a few questions you as a Muslim may wish to ask yourself:

1. If Jesus was replaced by someone else, when was he replaced? Was it before or after he was scourged? Was it immediately preceding his crucifixion?

2. Since, according to the Qur'an, he was replaced, why did no one notice he was replaced? Were the eyewitnesses so ignorant that they did not notice that the stripes on his back were no longer there? Was the best friend of Jesus, John the Beloved, so ignorant that he did not realize that the man he had walked with for three and a half years was not hanging on the cross in front of him? Was the very mother of Jesus so ignorant that she did not realize that the man hanging before her was not her own son?

3. Did Allah deliberately deceive Mary, the mother of Jesus, and John into believing that Jesus was dying on the cross? Or did

---

* Author Emir Caner's translation.

Allah simply allow these two people to go away from that dreadful day, never to know that Jesus was actually alive?

You may also want to ask yourself, "Do the sources outside the Qur'an and the Bible confirm the statements of either of the two books?" You will notice that even unbelievers such as Pliny the Younger,[2] the governor of Bithynia at the turn of the second century and a persecutor of Christians, and Josephus,[3] a Jew, acknowledge the death of Christ on the cross.

In the end, you must make the decision yourself. Our recommendation: read both the Qur'an and the Bible. Read passages on Christ such as suras 3–5 and the Gospel of John and then ask yourself the question, "Which do I believe?" Both sources promise to guide (sura 7:178; John 16:13), but only one promises to transform you (2 Corinthians 3:18) and declare you righteous (Romans 4:22).

In the end, the word *jihad*—which has become synonymous with bloodshed—also means to "struggle" or to "strive." As Muslim scholar Walid Phares writes in *Future Jihad,*

> While the concept of jihad was also applied to inner spiritual struggles adopted by individuals, it remained nevertheless under the overarching doctrine of historical jihad in the public sphere.[4]

In other words, though jihad was sometimes applied to inner struggle, the inner struggle was only in preparation for outward expressions of struggle and violent conflict.

In Islam, the ultimate jihad exchanges Muslim blood for Paradise. In fact, in much of the Muslim world, the idea that jihad is only an inner struggle and not an outward expression does not exist.

But if you wish to stop struggling, to stop striving, you can exchange Christ's death for your death and find life. His blood was shed for you. He exclaimed, "Come to me, all you who are weary and burdened, and I will give you rest" (Matthew 11:28). True surrender is not giving one's blood. True surrender is taking Christ's gift—a life without end (Hebrews 13:5).

Conclusion

24

What can you do if you are concerned about the future and your relationship with God?

If you have read what we have written about jihad and are worried or confused about the future, what can you do? Consider this: You can know that God has accepted you, forgiven you, and has given you eternal life. Jesus promises that all who believe on him can know that they *now* possess eternal life:

- "I tell you the truth, whoever hears my word and believes him who sent me *has eternal life* and will not be condemned; he has *crossed over* from death to life" (John 5:24).

- "Truly, truly, I say to you, he who believes has eternal life" (John 6:47 NASB).

Specifically, what does God want us to believe and trust in so we can have eternal life with him?

First, we must realize we have broken God's laws—if we were to die today, we would stand guilty before God and be eternally condemned. God bluntly states, "The soul who sins is the one who will die" (Ezekiel 18:4).

How can we know what sin is and if we have committed it? The Bible tells us, "For through the law comes the knowledge of sin" (Romans

3:20 NASB). The law would include the Ten Commandments and Jesus' Sermon on the Mount. A clear way to discover if we have broken God's law is found in Matthew 22. Jesus was asked,

> "Teacher, which is the greatest commandment in the law?" Jesus replied, "Love the Lord your God with all your heart and with all your soul and with all your mind. This is the first and greatest commandment. And the second is like it: 'Love your neighbor as yourself.' All the law and the prophets hang on these two commandments" (22:36-40).

Can any of us say we have loved God with all our heart, all our mind, and all our soul every moment we have lived? Would any of us tell God we had always loved our neighbor as we love ourselves? If we can't say yes to these two commands, then according to Jesus we are guilty of breaking the two greatest commandments God has given. We have sinned greatly! Further, we all know we are guilty of having committed other sins. This is a serious problem. The Bible says, "We know that whatever the law says, it says...so that every mouth may be silenced and the whole world held accountable to God" (Romans 3:19).

To solve this problem of lawbreaking and sin, all religions teach we must do certain things and keep certain laws. (For example, a Muslim must uphold the five pillars of Islam.) We are told to do this so we may perhaps merit God telling us, "You have done enough. I will give you Paradise because of what you have done." In Islam, for example, a person must outweigh his or her bad works by accumulating good works, hoping to achieve at least half good works. But even then, Islam teaches that a person may not make it.

Second, Christianity is the only religion in the world that teaches no man or woman can satisfy the requirements of God by what we might do. Rather, the Bible teaches God himself made the way for us to be forgiven. God sent his Son, Jesus, into the world to live a sinless, perfect life in order to provide for us the perfect righteousness we need to stand before God. Further, Jesus willingly died on the cross, where the sins of the world were placed on him. He experienced the full punishment of God that we deserve. In other words, he became our sin-bearer so that we need not be punished. God sent him to pay for our sins. This sounds too good to be true, but this is the good news of the gospel.

Where does the Bible teach that God sent Christ to pay the penalty for all our sins? The apostle Peter wrote, "Christ died for sins once for all, the righteous for the unrighteous, to bring you to God" (1 Peter 3:18). Jesus didn't have any sins of his own. He voluntarily became our substitute and died in our place. Everything that needed to be done to satisfy God's justice and holiness regarding our sin, Christ did for us while on the cross.

> "They all said, 'Are You the Son of God, then?' And He said to them, 'Yes, I am.'"

Jesus paid a debt we could never pay. Why? Because we committed our sins against an infinite, loving God, acts which deserve an infinite punishment. We couldn't pay an infinite punishment, but Jesus could. Jesus is the Son of God. Luke records this fact when describing one of Jesus' trials. "They all said, 'Are You the Son of God, then?' And He said to them, 'Yes, I am' " (Luke 22:70 NASB). As the Son of God, Jesus brought the good news that "God did not send his Son into the world to condemn the world, but to save the world through him" (John 3:17).

Where does the Bible teach that God credits the righteousness of Christ's perfectly lived life to our account so we can stand unblemished before God? Paul writes,

> To the man who does not work [that is, one who does not do good works to earn God's favor] but trusts God who justifies the wicked, his faith is credited as righteousness (Romans 4:5).

God credits to you the righteousness of Christ's sinless life the moment you place your faith in Christ. "This righteousness from God comes through faith in Jesus Christ to all who believe" (Romans 3:22).

Third, believing on Jesus is not just accepting facts about him. True belief is when you transfer all of your trust to Jesus to save you. When you do, you can know for certain you will go to heaven. Why?

Because the gift of salvation depends on Jesus living the perfect life, not you. Jesus already lived his perfect life and is now in heaven. The basis of our salvation is eternally secure.

We must realize we are all sinners and believe Jesus is the Son of God, that he lived a sinless life, that he died on the cross as a substitute for our sins, and then rose from the dead.

What does it mean to transfer all of our trust to Jesus and to believe in him to save us? Do you recall hearing a story about a man who walked across Niagara Falls on a tightrope? The crowd on the banks of the river was amazed. The man then proceeded to place 200 pounds of sandbags in a wheelbarrow and pushed the wheelbarrow across the falls. After doing this a few times, he finally spoke to the crowd and asked, "How many of you believe I can take this wheelbarrow across the falls again—with a person inside?" They all shouted they believed he could. Then he asked, "Which one of you will be the first to get in?"

Their belief he could do that was an intellectual faith, but trust would require them to get into the wheelbarrow. It's one thing to say you believe in Christ; it's another to entrust yourself into his hands. Would you be willing to right now put yourself into Christ's hands and ask him to forgive your sins and be your Savior and Lord? If you sincerely want to trust Jesus right now, you can do so by praying the following prayer to receive Jesus:

> *Dear Jesus,*
>
> *I acknowledge my sinfulness before you. I confess that I have been trying to earn my own salvation. But I now recognize my need for forgiveness and I understand that Christ died for my sins on the cross so I wouldn't have to be punished. I now trust in and receive you as my personal Savior and Lord. Come into my life, live in me, and give me courage and strength to face the opposition I may encounter. From this moment on, I will trust that you will take me to heaven when I die, as you promised. In Jesus' name I pray. Amen.*

Remember the promise of eternal life to those who believe:

God so loved the world that he gave his one and on̶
whoever believes in him shall not perish but have
For God did not send his Son into the world to c̶
world, but to save the world through him. Who
in him is not condemned, but whoever does not believe stands
condemned already because he has not believed in the name
of God's one and only Son (John 3:16-18).

I write these things to you who believe in the name of the
Son of God so that you may know that you have eternal life
(1 John 5:13).

If you have prayed to receive Christ, please write us at *The John Ankerberg Show* or e-mail us at thetruth@johnankerberg.org so we can send you some helpful materials about growing in the Christian life. We also recommend that you begin to read the New Testament to know more about the true Jesus Christ. In addition, attend a church that honors Christ as Lord and teaches the Bible as God's Word. Talk to God daily in prayer.

In addition, at www.johnankerberg.org we have video interviews available where we discuss many of the issues in this book in more detail together. You can preview a portion or order the programs to correspond with this book as part of a small group study.

For additional spiritual growth resources,
please visit our Web site at www.johnankerberg.org.

For more information about the ministry of Emir Caner,
please visit his Web site at www.emircaner.com.

Additional Resources on Islam

Additional important materials are available from the following organizations:

www.AlwaysBeReady.com: The Web site of speaker and author Charlie Campbell, which includes several Muslim articles and media resources.

www.Answering-Islam.org: Provides an in-depth historical and biblical response to doctrines of Islam and counters claims of Islamists. Includes an encyclopedia of Islam.

www.ApologeticsIndex.org: A huge directory of free apologetics resources featuring a quality overview of Islam with documented links.

www.BeThinking.org: Apologetics resources for free, with several specific to Islam, from a European Evangelical perspective.

www.CARM.org: The Christian Apologetics Resource Ministry (CARM) with a selection of short-answer articles on aspects of Islam as it relates to Christianity.

www.EmirCaner.com: A former Muslim turned Christian professor who is now president of Truett-McConnell College.

www.ErgunCaner.com: A former Muslim who is now a Christian and president of Liberty Baptist Theological Seminary.

www.ImpactApologetics.com: An online store representing a wide selection of apologetics-specific materials, including several audio downloads.

www.LeaderU.edu: This Campus Crusade for Christ resource offers an extensive array of academic articles on world religions, including many on Islam.

www.LeeStrobel.com: This Web site offers short video clips of leading scholars debating issues of Islam from a Christian perspective.

Notes

Section One—Introduction: The Question of Peace or Violence

1. Bukhari 9.58.
2. Samuel Zwemer, *The Law of Apostasy in Islam* (London: Marshall Brothers, Ltd., n.d.), 88.
3. Zwemer, 89.
4. www.fordham.edu/halsall/source/pact-umar.html.
5. www.persecution.com/topStory_saudiBrotherKilling.html.

Section Two—The Definition of Jihad in the Qur'an and the Traditions

1. Bernard Lewis, *The Crisis of Islam* (New York: Random House, 2004), 31.
2. Rudolph Peters, *Jihad in Classical and Modern Islam* (Princeton, NJ: Markus Wiener Publishers, 1996), 2.
3. Peters, 1.
4. Peters, 1.
5. Lewis, 30.
6. For a discussion on the Christian view of war, see Ergun and Emir Caner, *Christian Jihad* (Grand Rapids, MI: Kregel Publications, 2004), 216-227.
7. Lewis, 31.

Section Three—The Rules of Jihad

1. Stephen R. Hurst, "Mentally Retarded Women Used in Bombings," at www.breitbart.com/article .php?id=D8UHNN081&show_article=1.
2. A good illustration of this confusion can be seen through a recent declaration by the Saudi Minister of International Affairs, who clarified that jihad had to be promoted by a ruler. See www.arabnews .com/?page=1&section=0&article=9932&d=19&m=10&y=2001.
3. Averroës, "The Legal Qualifications on this Activity and the Persons Obliged to Take Part in It," *Al-Bidaya*, in Rudolph Peters, *Jihad in Classical and Modern Islam* (Princeton, NJ: Markus Wiener Publishers, 1996), 29.
4. Averroës. He quotes sura 48:17 as proof of his view.
5. David Jones, *Women Warriors: A History* (Washington, DC: Brassey's, Inc., 1997), 18-20.
6. Averroës, in Peters, 30.
7. See the seventh-century treaty, the Pact of Umar, for details about Jewish and Christian subjugation
8. Averroës, in Peters, 37.
9. Averroës, in Peters, 37-38.
10. For example, Muhammad limited Muslims to four wives (sura 4:3), while he married more than a dozen women. He argued that he received special revelation to do so (sura 33:50).
11. Ibn Warraq, *Why I Am Not a Muslim* (Amherst, NY: Prometheus Books, 1995), 219.
12. Warraq, 219.
13. Warraq, 220.
14. Peters, 34.
15. Barnabas Fund, "Islam and Slavery," *Barnabas Aid* (April-May 2007), www.answering-islam.org/ Green/slavery.htm.

Section Four—Muhammad's Understanding of Jihad

1. Robert Spencer, "Spencer: Cartoon Rage vs. Freedom of Speech," *FrontPage* (2 February 2006), at www.jihadwatch.org/archives/010009.php. For further discussion on this issue, see also Ergun and

Emir Caner, "Freedom and the Conscience of a Nation," *Unveiling Islam,* 2nd ed. (Grand Rapids, MI: Kregel Publications, 2009).

2. Muhammad Husayn Haykal, *The Life of Muhammad,* tr. Ismail al-Faruqi (Indianapolis: North American Trust Publications, 1976), 243. The book, in its entirety, can be found at www.witness-pioneer.org/vil/Books/MH_LM/default.htm.

3. Norman Geisler and Abdul Saleeb, *Answering Islam,* 2nd ed. (Grand Rapids, MI: Baker Books, 2002), 179.

4. William Montgomery Watt, *Muhammad: Prophet and Statesman* (Oxford: Oxford University Press, 1974), 112.

5. Ibn Ishaq, *The Life of Muhammad,* tr. Alfred Guillaume (Oxford: Oxford University Press, 1955), 288.

6. Ishaq, 288.

7. Geisler and Saleeb, 179. On another occasion Muhammad ordered the execution of another unbeliever by the name of Uqbah ibn Abu Muayt. When Uqbah pleaded for his life and expressed his concern for his children, Muhammad responded that "the fire" would take care of the children.

8. Robert Spencer, *The Politically Incorrect Guide to Islam (And the Crusades)* (Washington, DC: Regnery Publishing, 2005), 12.

9. Tor Andrae, *Muhammad: The Man and His Faith* (Mineola, NY: Dover Publications, 2000), 147-148.

10. James Arlandson, "Muhammad and the Massacre of the Qurayza Jews," *American Thinker* (25 February 2006), at www.americanthinker.com/2006/02/muhammad_and_massacre_of_the_q.html.

11. Alfred Guillaume, *Islam* (New York: Penguin Books, 1954), 47-48.

12. Ergun and Emir Caner, *Unveiling Islam* (Grand Rapids, MI: Kregel Publications, 2002), 50.

13. Caner, 51.

14. Winston Churchill, *The River War,* 1st ed., vol. 2 (London: Longmans, Green & Co., 1899), 248-250.

Section Five—Jihad As Carried Forward by Muhammad's Early Successors

1. "Al Maggari: Tarik's Address to His Soldiers," 711 CE, from *The Breath of Perfumes,* Medieval Sourcebook, at www.fordham.edu/halsall/source/711Tarik1.html.

2. "Al Maggari."

3. For an introductory article as to the progress of the Islamization of Europe, see Robert Spencer, "The Rapid Islamization of Europe," at www.worldnetdaily.com/news/article.asp?ARTICLE_ID=40504.

4. George W. Braswell Jr., *What You Need to Know about Islam and Muslims* (Nashville: Broadman and Holman Publishers, 2000), 47.

5. For a good introduction to Orthodox Christianity, see Timothy Ware, *The Orthodox Church* (London: Penguin Books, 1993).

6. "Accounts of the Arab Conquest of Egypt," *The History of the Patriarchs of Alexandria,* at Medieval Sourcebook.

7. Ergun and Emir Caner, *Unveiling Islam* (Grand Rapids: Kregel Publications, 2002), 69.

8. Caner, 70.

9. Caner, 70.

10. "The Prophet Muhammad's Last Sermon," at www.fordham.edu/halsall/source/muhm-sermon.html.

11. W. Montgomery Watt and Pierre Cachia, *A History of Islamic Spain* (Edinburgh: Edinburgh University Press, 1965), 9-12. Also see Kenneth Baxter Wolf, *Christian Martyrs in Muslim Spain* (Cambridge: Cambridge University Press, 1988), at http://libro.uca.edu/martyrs/martyrs.htm.

12. "Medieval Sourcebook: Arabs, Franks, and the Battle of Tours, 732: Three Accounts," at www

.fordham.edu/halsall/source/732tours.html. Also Edward Shepherd Creasy, *Decisive Battles of the World* (Colonial Press, 1899).

13. Many argue that Otto I (AD 962) was the first emperor of the official empire, but its formation unquestionably finds its roots and power in Charlemagne.

14. The term *free-church Christians* is defined as those who would not submit to the state-sponsored church, the Roman Church. Examples in medieval history include the Albigensians, Petrobrusians, and Waldensians.

Section Six—Jihad from Islam's Greatest Years to the Present

1. Robert Siegel, "Sayyid Qutb's America," at www.npr.org/templates/story/story.php?storyId=1253796.

2. Siegel.

3. Bernard Lewis, *The Crisis of Islam* (New York: Random House, 2004), 78-79.

4. Lewis, 80.

5. For a good treatment of the shift in power, see Kirk H. Sowell, *The Arab World: An Illustrated History* (New York: Hippocrene Books, 2004).

6. Linda S. George, *The Golden Age of Islam* (New York: Benchmark Books, 1998), 8.

7. Muslim's Hadith parallels Bukhari on these punishments: amputation for thievery (Muslim 17.4175) and stoning for adultery (Muslim 17.4194).

8. "October 2, 1187: Saladin Captures Jerusalem from the Crusaders," *Christian History* magazine, at http://chi.gospelcom.net/DAILYF/2001/10/daily-10-02-2001.shtml.

9. For example, Chatillon, a Christian crusader general, executed several dozen Muslims for simply trespassing on Christian property. Chatillon was himself executed at the hands of Saladin. See the article in footnote 7 for further detail.

10. Bat Ye'or, *The Dhimmi: Jews and Christians under Islam* (Madison, NJ: Fairleigh Dickinson University Press, 1985), 71.

11. Ye'or, 117.

12. Sahih Muslim 19.4363, emphasis adeed.

13. For a list of patriarchs according to the Eastern Orthodox Church, see www.cc-pair.org/list/index.php?lang=en.

14. Philip Mansel, *Constantinople: City of the World's Desire* (New York: St. Martin's Griffin, 1998), at www.washingtonpost.com/wp-srv/style/longterm/books/chap1/constantinople.htm

15. M. J. Akbar, *The Shade of Swords: Jihad and the Conflict Between Islam and Christianity* (New York: Routledge, 2003), 86.

16. Akbar, 86-87.

17. www.pbs.org/wgbh/pages/frontline/shows/saudi/analyses/wahhabism.html.

Section Seven—Our Response to Jihad

1. See Emir Fethi Caner, "Islam and Christianity," in Paul Copan and William Lane Craig, eds., *Passionate Conviction: Contemporary Discourses on Christian Apologetics* (Nashville: Broadman and Holman Publishers, 2007), 202-204.

2. See original letter at www.pbs.org/wgbh/pages/frontline/shows/religion/maps/primary/pliny.html.

3. See original letter by Josephus in both Arabic and Greek at ccat.sas.upenn.edu/~humm/Topics/JewishJesus/josephus.html.

4. Walid Phares, *Future Jihad: Terrorist Strategies Against the West* (New York: Palgrave Macmillan, 2005), 45.

About the Authors

John Ankerberg, host of the award-winning *John Ankerberg Show,* has three earned degrees: a Master of Arts in church history and the philosophy of Christian thought, a Master of Divinity from Trinity Evangelical Divinity School, and a Doctor of Ministry from Luther Rice Seminary. He has coauthored the two-million-selling Facts On series of apologetic books, as well as *Middle East Meltdown* and *What's the Big Deal About Other Religions?*

Emir Caner was disowned by his devout Muslim father, a mosque leader, when he believed in Christ. He turned his studies toward history and Christian theology, earning his PhD in history. Recently he was selected as president of Truett-McConnell College (Cleveland, Georgia). Coauthor with his brother Ergun of the bestselling *Unveiling Islam* and numerous other books, he travels worldwide and makes many media appearances to speak about Jesus Christ.

Also in
The Truth About Islam Series

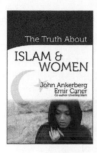

THE TRUTH ABOUT ISLAM AND WOMEN
John Ankerberg and Emir Caner

As the son of a devout mosque leader, immersed in the Islamic worldview, Emir Caner offers you the real picture of women under Islam. He and John Ankerberg delve under the claims of Muslim apologists and help open your eyes to...

- the conditions of near slavery women suffer in many Islamic cultures
- Muhammad's ambivalence toward females
- the contempt for women found in the Qur'an and the Muslim Traditions
- the basis for women's subjugation in Islam's teachings
- the dehumanizing double standard regarding men's and women's sexual behavior

Ankerberg and Caner leave no doubt why, in the light of history, *Christianity* is the truly radical religion regarding the treatment and status of women. A great source for understanding and discussion.

To read a sample chapter of these or other Harvest House books,
go to www.harvesthousepublishers.com

Other Helpful Harvest House Resources

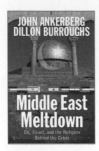

MIDDLE EAST MELTDOWN
Oil, Israel, and the Religion Behind the Crisis
John Ankerberg and Dillon Burroughs

News headlines from the war-torn Middle East are constantly changing, making it hard to understand the causes of the conflict in that part of the world and how it affects us. This clear guide to a complex situation answers these urgent questions:

- Why does peace continue to elude the Arab nations and Israel?
- What part does Middle East oil play?
- Where do Iran, Lebanon, and Hezbollah fit into the big picture?
- What can we expect from today's new breed of terrorists?
- What does the United States have at stake?

Featuring exclusive interviews with today's top religious scholars and extensive journalistic research, this fast-paced and user-friendly resource points to the root of the problem and reveals how today's events fit into God's plan for the future.

SEARCHING FOR THE ORIGINAL BIBLE
Who Wrote It and Why? • Is It Reliable? • Has the Text Changed over Time?
Randall Price

Lost...destroyed...hidden...forgotten. For many centuries, no one has seen any of the original biblical documents. How can you know whether today's Bible is true to them?

Researcher and archaeologist Randall Price brings his expert knowledge of the Bible to tackle crucial questions:

- What happened to the original Bible text? If we don't have it, what *do* we have?
- How was the text handed down to our time? Can you trust that process?
- What about the Bible's claim to be inspired and inerrant?

Current evidence upholds the Bible's claim to be the authoritative record of God's revelation—a Book you can build your life and faith on.